A Short Introduction to SAKTA PHILOSOPHY

AF825339

SHORT INTRODUCTION series comprises of quality reference books which are for everyone wanting an interesting and easy-to-understand gateway to a new subject. They are written by experts with complete command of the subject.

Other similar **INDIGO BOOKS** available (or to be published shortly) are:

A SHORT INTRODUCTION TO VAISNAVISM

A SHORT INTRODUCTION TO SAIVISM

A SHORT INTRODUCTION TO INDIAN MUSIC

A SHORT INTRODUCTION TO MIMANSA

A SHORT INTRODUCTION TO SANKHYA

A SHORT INTRODUCTION TO VEDANTA

A SHORT INTRODUCTION TO SIX SYSTEMS OF INDIAN PHILOSOPHY

A SHORT INTRODUCTION TO INDIAN ARCHAEOLOGY

A SHORT INTRODUCTION TO INDIAN WORSHIP

A SHORT INTRODUCTION TO YOGA PHILOSOPHY

A Short Introduction to SAKTA PHILOSOPHY

Subodh Kapoor

Editor of THE HINDUS. Encyclopaedia of Hinduism, in 5 volumes
THE BUDDHISTS. Encyclopaedia of Buddhism, in 5 volumes
Encyclopaedia of Indian Heritage, in 90 volumes
Encyclopaedia of Vedic Philosophy, in 9 volumes
Encyclopaedia of Indian Philosophers, in 9 volumes
The Indian Encyclopaedia, in 25 volumes

INDIGO BOOKS

AN
INDIGO BOOK
PUBLISHED BY INDIGO BOOKS
Paperback division of
COSMO PUBLICATIONS,
24-B, Ansari Road, Darya Ganj,
New Delhi 110 002, India.

INDIGO BOOKS and
COSMO PUBLICATIONS
are wholly owned subsidiaries of
GENESIS PUBLISHING PVT. LTD.,
New Delhi, India

A SHORT INTRODUCTION TO SAKTA PHILOSOPHY

Copyright © 2002 INDIGO BOOKS

First INDIGO Edition 2002

ISBN 81-291-0013-4

This book is sold subject to the condition that it shall not, by way of trade or otherwise, be lent, re-sold, hired out or otherwise circulated without the publisher's prior consent in any form of binding or cover other than that in which this is published and without a similar condition including this condition being imposed on the subsequent purchaser.

ALL RIGHTS RESERVED

PRINTED AND BOUND IN INDIA

Contents

Introduction

The Indian Religion of the Goddess Shakti

During the three years which I spent in India I had the good fortune to travel in many different parts of that vast territory, both east, north, west, and south, visiting in turn the Shan States in Burma, Kashmir, the west coast of Bombay, and Southern India and Ceylon. There were two things which from a spiritual point of view attracted my attention most, and these were the type of Buddhism prevailing in Burma and Ceylon, and that special branch of Indian religion and philosophy, almost unknown in its essence in Europe, called the Religion of the Goddess Shakti, which flourishes in Bengal and Kashmir. Personal contact with many Indian friends, whose acquaintance I had the pleasure to make, gave me the chance of studying Indian spiritual thought more deeply and, if I may say so, in a more live manner than it is possible to do from books only, even if they are old Sanskrit texts. I was honoured by an invitation from the Indian Philosophical Congress at Calcutta in 1925 and at Benares in 1926 to deliver lectures. There, while staying for some time with Indian friends with whom I was in sympathy by reason of a certain similarity in our spiritual-philosophical researches, I realised the strength and depth of eastern spiritual thought.

My object here is to give you a short Introduction to the particular branch of Indian spiritual thought, the religion of the Goddess Shakti, which is still unknown in its true meaning in Europe and, I must say, even in the greater part of India. What I have read about it in the different books on Indian philosophy have been only simple and short allusions, containing more often than not rather erroneous ideas. In that excellent work on *Hinduism and Buddhism*, by Sir Charles Eliot, there are only a few remarks on Shaktism, as this religion is usually called, and these describe its deep philosophy and ritualism in a way which cannot be regarded as altogether impartial. The European attitude towards this religious system seems to me to be much influenced by not particularly well informed opponents of it, from whom, I imagine, Sir Charles Eliot has gathered his information. That is understandable because, as he himself remarks in a footnote, the new text books of Shaktism, which have been published by Arthur Avalon, were at that time not available to him. These text books, which include introductions and philosophic foundation to this religious system and throw an illuminating light on this very important branch of human thought, I have the privilege to be personally acquainted with and, I may add, to be a friend of that Indian personality, Arthur Avalon, the editor of the text books of Shaktism, who from modesty, and following an old and good Indian tradition, is hiding his personal name under the above pseudonym. There are now, I believe, over twenty volumes, including the most important *Maha Nirvana Tantra*, which means the Philosophy of the Great Liberation, were published under the patronage and with the financial assistance of the then great Maharaja of Mithila on the borders of Bengal. It is good to know that there are in India men like this Maharaja, whom I had the pleasure to meet personally and who spends a good part of his great fortune in furthering the revival of the spiritual influence of Shaktism, to which he personally adheres.

In making an attempt to describe to you Shaktism, my

object is to present you with a sketch of the metaphysical aspect of the religion as compared with other systems of philosophical thought. It is not my intention here to dwell on the ritual and ceremonial aspect of the religion.

The expression, Shaktism is derived from the word "Shakti." The word Shakti means "Power" both latent and manifest. When personalised it means the Devi of Power; she is Deva. The Devi Shakti is the power aspect of the supreme spirit. The doctrines and ritual of Shaktism are contained in a special branch of the holy Scriptures of India, called *Tantra Shastra*, which acknowledges the authority of the great Veda. "Veda" means the God inspired word which has from the oldest times been the foundation of Indian spiritual thought and culture; but it is not confined to what is called the four Vedas. They are but parts of it and based on the one Veda—for 'Vak' or 'Logos' is one.

Shaktism is an eminently practical religion. Practically the whole content of its scriptures consists in rules and ritual by which the higher realisation of the spiritual truth may be gained. This way of personal spiritual attainment, or Yoga, which is known to all Indian religions, is called in Shaktism, Sadhana. Very often the remark can be found in the Tantrik texts that by merely pondering about the husks of words nothing is done, *i.e.*, mere book-knowledge is useless—but that only by practically touching the truth itself can liberation, bliss and the highest consciousness be won.

This truth, to which Shaktism is devoted with all its energy, is represented by the conception of the goddess Shakti. Such a conception, that truth unveils itself spiritually in a female aspect, can only be grasped with difficulty by the European mind. The European mind is not accustomed to see differences between male and female in the spiritual world, and finds them only as far as physical sexual differences can still be discerned. But the idea of a female quality of the spirit has always been known to the deeper minds of humanity and stretches through the whole inner history of culture. Leaving aside the cults of aboriginal tribes, animism, etc., there may be mentioned, in addition to the Goddess Shakti of Indian culture, the conception of Isis in the Egyptian religion, of the figure Kwannon in China, the idea of Eve in Babylonian times and many others leading up to that connected with the Madonna of the Roman Catholic Church. Certainly there are very interesting and important differences in all these great conception; but it would go too far here to treat of this special subject. It is mentioned only to show that female spirituality has always played an important role in human thought.

The Goddess Shakti is the "power" which pervades the whole of the universe, and from which the Universe has emanated. There is nothing within the manifest world which is not Shakti in its essence. The manifest world is mind and matter, that is to say, all that we call our thought, will, imagination, etc. is mind, and all the realm of nature is matter. She—in her highest aspect—is pure spirit or pure consciousness—as such she is called Chit-Shakti—but her nature and essence become apparent also in all that we are aware of through our senses. So She is matter—substance too—and as such She is called Maya-Shakti. Here is no antagonism between the spiritual and the natural sides of the universe, since she is both of them.

In order to illustrate more clearly this important principle of Shaktism. I would like to compare it with the structure of other philosophical systems in Europe or India. It may be said that all the great and well-known philosophical expressions of human thought are either monistic or dualistic, that is to say, have as their basis one or two original eternal units. Let me show it in a diagrammatic way. The dualistic view presupposes two basic units, Mind and Matter:

Both of these are absolute and ultimate, and everything can be derived from either of them; whereas monism takes either mind or matter as the single existing principle, of which the other is only an appearance, a different aspect or a mere effect. Taking mind as such a principle, the expression is called "Spiritual Monism", meaning that the Spirit is the ultimate true reality and all the material world is an "illusion" or its effect, issuing from it (a downward line would indicate this); on the other hand, regarding matter as the only basic ultimate reality, mind and spirit have no substance of their own and are mere products of matter, which could be shown by a line going upwards. Now Shaktism is something quite different from the denominations of Monism and Dualism, in so far as Shakti lies behind both mind and matter, without giving preponderance to either of them. Mind and matter as represented by the created universe are Shakti, and Shakti is bound up with Shiva, the male spiritual element whose position in the system it is difficult to describe to the European mind, but who may be taken to represent the inert Spirit lying apart from, and unconnected with, the Universe, but whose touch is necessary to give to Shakti the impulse to create. Both of them, female universal Power, Shakti, and the male impulse-giver, Shiva, constitute therefore the spiritual background of the Universe. Thus in terms of philosophical thought Shaktism is neither wholly dualistic nor wholly monistic, but constitutes a monistic dualism or dualistic monism, a "two in one" or "one in two".

The follower of Shaktism, the worshipper of Shakti, is called Shaktá. His conception of the Goddess is described in the Shakti Tantra Shastras, *i.e.*, the holy scriptures of Shaktism, often in a very poetical way. Whereas we speak of Mother Nature only in a comparative manner, for the Shakta it is absolute reality. Nature is Her body. Her presence is personally felt by him, when he is standing on the fertile ground of the earth; he touches Her life in the blossoms of the pure lotus-flower. She animates all living creatures. His own body is a part of Her great body. Worshipping Her in all Her different forms, he will find Her light, too, within his mind and consciousness. Thus, to the Shakta the whole universe of mind and matter reveals itself in its unity; he see before him Her great body which he adores; Her sacred feet, Her heart, Her mind.

It might be useful to describe this poetical view, which is at once physical and transcendental, by means of another diagram. We may for this purpose represent matter and mind by two circles which intersect each other like this:

Where they intersect, there is Shakti, so to speak, in Herself. But Her influence, Her being spreads into the whole realm of matter as well as that of mind. Nowhere is She absent, but Her presence is less distinct, is somehow veiled in those parts which are further from the center, where She is in Herself. Thus, for the sake of linear explanation, the mineral world—the solid matter—would have to be situated the furthest from Her, because there, as for instance in stone, she—Life Herself—is, much veiled, stone to the ordinary human view appearing to be dead. Nearer to Her is the realm of plants, where, with their growing and blossoming, She already becomes more apparent. I need hardly remind you of the well-known researches by Sir Jagadis Bhose of the University of Calcutta, who is endeavouring to make visible the actual heart-beat of plant life. Then, in due order with regard to Her would come the world of animals, which being animated have within their life—although perhaps still unconsciously—some access to Her. Lastly, within the highly developed organism of man She, for the first time, is inherent in her essential being. There She finds the possibility of being consciously awakened, so that she appears to him, who is looking and striving for her, in Her true nature as Shakti herself. The other side—the mind circle—comprises the mental faculties of man such as consciousness, will, feeling and logical perception, which, with regard to their aptitude for Her realisation, may be put in such order. The directions of development therefore go in the matter-circle from left to right—from stone, vegetable, animal to man, where Shakti will be realised; in the mind-circle, from right to left—from mere logical thinking to feeling, will-power, consciousness to man—where Shakti may be realised. Thus, as you can see from this diagram, everywhere there is Shakti. She is inherent in everything and at the same time transcends every thing; by meditation and religious ceremonies She may be realized everywhere, being inherent in the whole physical universe as it is given to us. And, moreover, above this we may touch Her in Her transcendental aspect as well. When She appears in Her true nature, then there is no more mind or matter, but only She Herself, in no sense bounded by such limitations. As such a one She may well be represented by a circle, the universe in its true aspect.

To the European it may perhaps at first sight appear to be a mere poetical presentment and but little different from the theory of vitalism of modern natural science or from ancient animism in the religious aspect. But with regard to Vitalism, even if there be similarities the essential difference seems to me, that the Vitalism of the natural sciences is based principally upon the conception of a material world which is regarded as being animated by, for instance, the "lan vitale" of Bergson. But Shatism holds its standpoint entirely on the spiritual side. She, the great mother, exists, and what in the material world is vitalised or animated, certainly comes from Her, but is only a veiled appearance of Her, who in Her true being can be experienced spiritually. And Shaktism is also not animism, if by animism may be understood the primitive idea of everything being ghostlike, being animated by "Phi" or spirits, resulting in as many ghostly spirits as there are different things. Shaktism represents a spiritual unity, all different things being united within Her always greater aspect.

The principal doctrine of "Shaktism", that the whole Universe of mind and matter is created by Her, the Powerful Goddess Shakti, is described in full detail, with Indian accuracy in spiritual matters, in the Cosmogony of Shaktism. It must be understood that every great Indian philosophical system has its own Cosmo-Genesis, that is, its special conception of the evolution of the world and its beginning. As a matter of fact, every conception of life and the Universe requires such a foundation to give it the necessary firm hold. For Shaktism this source, out of which the Universe as mind and matter has evolved, is the female spiritual Power, Shakti, who is the Great Mother of the Universe. In Her most concentrated form, when Her Power is just ready to expand, She is represented by a point called Bindu. This Bindu Point is mere Spirit. Everything manifested and created in this Universe has Spirit. Everything manifested and created in this Universe has Spirit as its source and essence. In the Christian Cosmo-Genesis of the Gospel of St. John it is called "logos" or "the word". By expansion the Spiritual Power Shakti becomes, going through many different stages, Mind, Life, and Matter. She—the Goddess—is contained, in all the manifestations of the universe, but She remains, so to speak, unexhausted by being the material cause of the Universe. She in Her essence remains unaffected and greater than all the created world.

In a diagrammatic way this cosmogenetic evolution can be represented like this. The active, most concentrated Point Bindu is red, the colour of activity. From this point the lines of evolution expand through the stages of mind and life towards matter, the mineral world. So the material world stands not first but last in the evolution of the Universe.

According to the general doctrine of Indian metaphysics, this whole created universe is not everlasting but will one day be dissolved. The life or appearance of the universe lasts, as it is figuratively expressed, one day of Brahma, the Almighty, that is, millions and millions of years. After that the whole expansion contracts again in the opposite direction; first, matter will be dissolved, then life and mind will disappear till it reaches the state of the beginning, the spiritual Point, Bindu, where it will find its rest; until the dawn of a new day of Brahma, when a new creation will start. This Bindu Point is the great Goddess, the universal mother—womb—yoni—the creator and receiver of the Universe, which, as Shakti, is worshipped by the followers of Shaktism.

So the whole created world has as its creative Power Shakti, the goddess, just as in this world the female element is constantly maintaining it. But She, the creative Goddess, can do nothing without Him, the God, Shiva, just as no woman can bear fruit without the co-operation of the male element. The relation of Shakti to Shiva, is of a very subtle, spiritual nature. He, Shiva is in contrast to all creation, be it mind or matter. He is the underlying pure consciousness which is independent of, and superior to, all creation. In a very famous picture of Shaktism the goddess Shakti stands black-coloured on the white-coloured Shiva who lies inert. The symbolism is this. Shiva is white to represent a colourless form, since all colours belong to the created world, which is the domain of Shakti. He lies at absolute rest, since movement and activity belong to the created world, which is dependent on him, but not he on it, She, the Goddess, is black-coloured because, compared with the light of the spiritual world unmixed with any objective realisation, she is dark as the night; in all creation she is veiled in darkness, both her face and her raiment.

One of the deepest secrets of Shaktism is the union of the highest spiritual male consciousness, Shiva, with the all-pervading female power, Shakti. As I have already mentioned, the all-powerful Shakti would not be able to create the universe out of Herself; She needs the touch of Shiva. This union of Shiva and Shakti takes place in the highest spiritual regions before anything has been created, so to speak, in the night of Brahma. Out of this union the Universe is born—Shakti evolves as mind and matter, whereas Shiva remains as the underlying background, unaltered, This highest spiritual state of union is inexpressible by words; but it is approximately circumscribed by the Sanskrit words; Sat—Chit—Ananda. Sat means Being; Chit means Consciousness, and when these are united with one another, there Ananda—Bliss—the highest spiritual bliss, is the issue. For the Shakta, as for the Hindu generally, the essence of the world is joy, bliss, ananda. Whenever truth, living truth, is approached or touched by man, then he feels that bliss of the union of Shiva and Shakti which is the origin of all life. The highest state of consciousness or liberation (Mukti) in Shaktism is the attainment, the spiritual realisation, of the highest, unchanging, eternal, absolute union of Shiva and Shakti within himself, into which his being is to be ultimately absorbed. The man who has realised this and transplanted himself into it is in his lifetime called Jivanmukta (liberated though living). In this union is everything essential contained.

But within space and time, within the world of separate things and forms,—in this world of limited experience in which we are living—this highest union is interrupted. Shakti, being separated from Him, is, so to speak, in Her actual body distributed among all objective experience.

There is a deep and striking picture, a story of Indian mythology, which tells how the body of Shakti has been dismembered and has fallen in pieces into this world. Wherever any part of Her holy body is supposed to be lying, there an Indian temple has been built; to a certain extent comparable to the Stupas which are erected by Buddhists for the relies of the sacred body of Gautama. Everything in the objective appearance is individual on account of its being separated from that union, and its material substance or embodiment can be measured by the interval of that separation; the further away from the union, the more its spiritual essence is veiled.

It follows consequently that in every individual being, which to a certain extent becomes conscious of itself, there must be living a tendency to become liberated from this separation, to come back to this primordial union. "Back to the mother", it may be said, is the shortest expression for the spiritual aim of the whole of Indian culture and especially of Shaktism. A deeply—felt longing prevails within the religious mind of India; a longing like that of a child for its mother. It is important to note this, since it is this longing which gives the impulse to the means by which the aim of coming back to the Mother may be attained. These means are called the Yoga of Shaktism, *i.e.*, Sadhana. The principles of Yoga are almost the same in all the different Indian systems, of which they form an essential part. By urging concentration of thought upon certain important ideas, they aim at giving to these ideas more strength and clearness than they usually have. The meditator excludes himself from all outer influences, in order to bring his mind into direct contact with the spiritual world. In the end he will eventually realise what his Scriptures have taught him, that his essence is Spirit, and his mind and body its manifestations. I may mention here that a modern "western" way of "Yoga" has been introduced into Europe by the spiritual system, "Anthroposophy", of Dr.Rudolf Steiner. In all ages such kinds of spiritual endeavour have been practised. If man succeeds in actually realising the inner meaning of metaphysics, he becomes, as it is called, "initiated", that is, he becomes a citizen of the spiritual world, just as he is a citizen of the natural world by his physical birth. The Yoga of Shaktism specializes in conceptions of the Goddess Shakti. If She appears to the Shakta, as She is in Herself, the highest realisation, the Union with the mother is attained. Then the Shakta says: She I am, and feels himself full of the greatest spiritual bliss.

As I have already mentioned, Shaktism is an eminently practical Religion. It attempts an immediate realisation of truth by the practical methods of "Yoga" and has an abundance of rites and ceremonies. These vary according to the competency of the Shakta. The ritual has been rightly called the Art of Religion. The worshipper follows certain prescribed rules in his adoration, which give him the right direction. Every Religion knows the value of ritual—Buddhism as well as Christianity and Shaktism. I may mention here only a few special points, which distinguish the rites from all other similar cults in India.

It is well known what an important role the caste-system has always played in India. Even now the distinctions of the different castes are much observed, especially in the case of marriage. Principally the Brahmins, as the caste of priests—now there are Brahmins who are doctors of medicine, barristers, watchmen, etc.,—would never mix with other castes in their ritual worship. The Shakta, however, the worshipper of Shakti, does not pay any regard to these caste distinctions. The Brahma Shakta has no objection to worshipping the Goddess even with the Shudra outcast, the Pariah. Such a non-Indian uncommon attitude shows that the rites of Shaktism may have their source from abroad; it is not yet quite certain, but it is probable that the special rites of Shaktism have come to India from China through Tibet.

This would explain, too, the other striking feature of the Shakta-worship, which is also non-Indian—that during the ritual worship of Shakti it is allowed to eat meat and to drink wine. Everyone knows how the Hindus abhor the slaughter of animals; how the adoration of the cow is an essential part of their religion, which has been again and again emphasised, especially by Gandhi himself. The Shaktá, however, eats meat and drinks wine during his worship of the Goddess Shakti. He feels himself spiritually above this custom. As in his view everything is She—the Goddess—

there can be made no exception with regard to the offerings to Her.

The third unique quality of the Shakti-worship is the active participation of women in the ceremonies. Ordinarily women are always kept apart in India. Everyone has heard of the Purdah system, which holds in some parts of India the women-folk life-long in their houses. But the Shakta treats them as altogether equal; even more. She, his Wife, is regarded by him as his Shakti Goddess; She, the mother of his children, represents to him the Great Mother. Such an attitude is naturally reflected in the daily life of Shakti Hindu families, where the mother—quite contrary to Miss Mayo's statements in *Mother India*—is much venerated. There is the so-called Panchatattva Ritual—the most important ritual of Shaktism, which is still nowadays performed in Bengal. The name "Panchatattva" is derived from the words "Pancha", five, and "Tattva", elements. The five elements of this ritual are Wine, Meat, Fish, Parched Corn and Sexual Union. Men and women meet as equal partners. They sit together—the man beside the women—in a circle, called Chakra. Following elaborate rites, they offer to the Goddess wine, meat, fish and corn. After that they take their meal, which consists these four elements; the idea being that they unite themselves with Shakti in these products and fruits. The highest presentment of the Goddess for the Shakta is the women who is sitting by his side. By uniting with her—according to the Maithuna rites—he experiences the bliss of the great union of Shiva and Shakti. Pro-creation is the individual counterpart of Cosmic Creation. It must be understood that the purpose of the physical union of the Shakta with his Shakti in this ritual is not satisfaction of his physical senses but the spiritual realisation of the highest union of the individual with the Goddess, the Cosmic-Whole. It may be mentioned that, as far as I have heard, during the ceremonies in Bengal the last mentioned Maithuna rites are not actually performed but are only indicated, as for example by bowing to the woman sitting at his side in the Chakra. Nothing is wrong or forbidden according to Shaktism, if it is done with a pure heart and spiritual feeling. Certainly it is possible that, weak as man's nature is, abuses of this special rite have taken place—and it would be wrong to deny that they are in fact happening. But my intention here is to show its spiritual meaning and intention; which, in my opinion, cannot be affected by abuse in its interpretation; and the principle of the rite is sound, grand and spiritual.

All the rites of Shaktism, of which I have here mentioned only one, tend in such a direction as to awaken within him the spiritual and aesthetically productive forces of man. As soon as these usually slumbering forces are awakened, the Shakta knows and feels himself as being born again within the spiritual world. The Shakta says, "As I am born in my physical body from my mother, so I must be spiritually born again from my spiritual mother, the Goddess Shakti." By the grace of Shakti the Shakta himself becomes Brahma. As a matter of fact, every spiritual man strives for the attainment of such a state, of being reborn in the spiritual sense. Only the expressions are different and the means and ways vary. In Shaktism it is striking to notice with what absoluteness and how independently of all other systems of religion the physical appearance and the highest spiritual realisation are combined together. If Shakti is everywhere, then she is, too, in the bodily appearance of the women and there, however veiled, in her fullest essence. So he makes use of her for the greatest spiritual aim of man, namely to be reborn by the grace of Shakti.

Now I have said that this aim of being reborn within the spiritual motherhood is known to almost every religion, and, althought Buddhism in its fundamental basis at first seems to be utterly different from Shaktism, yet Northern Buddhism knows well what is meant by Shakti. Mahayana

Buddhism, as it is prevalent in Tibet, by which country Shaktism too has been much influenced, has introduced into its system during its development the Goddess Tara. She represents what Shakti is for Shaktism. She is the embodiment of all that within the spiritual realisation is distinctly female; and it is a very secret saying in esoteric Northern Buddhism that man, by being reborn from Tara, will become a Buddha, that is, will attain the highest spiritual state of life to which man is destined and for which he is striving.

As a matter of fact, the female spiritual element as it is venerated by Shaktism, being a living truth, can to a certain extent become a combining factor to embrace the great cultural outlook both of the East and the West. Humanity is one over all the earth, and Womanhood is its essential part. In Shaktism the idea of the spiritual creative force of Womanhood finds its most absolute and exclusive expression. For this reason this system is so interesting and striking for anyone who takes the trouble to go more deeply into it. Shakti, as she is pleased to reveal herself to-day, is present, too, within the depths of European culture. It would take me too far a field to prove it by further details. I would only mention that Goethe concludes his great poem, "Faust", with the words: "The eternal female is raising us". Certainly, Goethe had no knowledge of the system of Shaktism and of those texts which we are now privileged to study. But by his poetical inspiration he touched by himself the truth which we find so clearly expressed in the system of Shaktism. If one would try to express the deepest meaning which Shaktism may have for us in our days, it cannot be done better than by those words which the mystical chorus sings at the end of this great poem: *Das Ewig Weibliche zieht uns hinan.* "The eternal female is raising us".

DR. HANS KOESTER

one

Śakti in the Upa-Purāṇas

The Upa-Purāṇas

The *Upa-Purāṇas* are valuable records of Indian life and thought, but it is a matter of great surprise that very little has been known about these. Scholars never cared to peep into these works, by saying that these are sectarian works. The work done by a few scholars on the *Upa-purāṇas* is of very little importance. It is only Dr. R.C. Hazra, who very recently has worked hard to study the *Upa-purāṇic* lore, the hidden treasure of the cultural and religious life in Ancient and medieval India. He has published two volumes on '*The studies in the Upa-purāṇas*'. These volumes have been helpful in revealing the importance of the *Upa-purāṇas* literature before the learned world. These *Upa-purāṇas* afford us great insight into all phases and aspects of Hinduism viz.its mythology, philosophy, festivals, ceremonies, and its ethics. These works supply us with important information about the different branches of science and literature, developed in ancient India.[1] In these respects, these are rather more important than the *Mahā-purāṇas*. The *Upa-purāṇas* attained an authoritative position from an early date; among the sactaries of different sects and the writers of *Nibandhas*, on the topics varying from details on ceremonies to moral works of daily life.

NUMBER

Following the tradition of the *Mahā-purāṇas*, orthodox opinion tries to limit the number of the *Upa-purāṇas* rigidly to eighteen, even in those cases, where the promulgators of such opinion are fully conscious of the existence of a large number .[2] While in the enumerations of the *Purāṇas* there is almost complete agreement with regard to the titles, this is by no means the case with the titles of the *Upa-purāṇas*. It has been very clearly pointed out by R.C. Hazra who produced the different lists of the titles of the *Upa-purāṇas*.[3] He has mentioned 23 lists,[4] found in the various *Purāṇas* or *Upa-purāṇas*, generally quoted by the *Nibandhakaras*, showing their divergency over the titles of the *Upa-Purāṇas*. Besides the *Upa-Purāṇas* mentioned, in these lists there are many others, either in printed form, or in manuscripts, or known from references and quotations. We can only say that the *Upa-Purāṇas* are very rich in number, amounting not less than one hundred.

DATE

Though there may be some *Upa-Purāṇas* of later dates but it is definite on the basis of accepting them as anthority by the *Nibandhakāras*[5], that the group of the *Upa-Purāṇas* cannot be dated later than 850 A.D. As the mention of the titles of the *Upa-purāṇas* has been made in the *Mahāpurāṇas* -viz. *Kūrma Purāṇa* the *Matsya Purāṇa,* only mentioning four *Sūta Saṁhītā* or *Skanda Purāṇa*, *Garuḍa*, *Purāṇa, Devī Bhāgavata Purāṇa*; the date of formation of the group may be placed appoximately between 650 and 800 A.D.[6] But this cannot limit the scope of early origin of the *Upa-purāṇic* literature. It is not possible to place all the works in one date because they deal with different sects and their nature and contents differ widely. We may find the references and traces of the scattered *Upa-purāṇic* works developing and originating in the end of the Gupta period.[7] The *Matsya Purāṇa* considers the *Upa-puranas* as mere sub-sections of the *Puranas*; this view is widely accepted in the *Puraṇas* themselves and by the *Nibandhkāras*.

Just like the *Purāṇas,* the *Upa-purāṇas* are also said to have five characteristics viz. creation, recreation, genealogy of gods, Kings and sages, Manu-periods of time, and history of the royal dynasties as well as the families of sages.[8] But the *Upa-purāṇic* literature is more exclusively adopted to suit the purposes of local cults and the religious needs of different sects than the *Mahā-purāṇas,* and arose at a time when the genealogies began to be neglected, and is never serious about these five characteristies. These works altogether neglect the genealogies of the kings and sages. If at all these works mention some important names of the kings, no care is taken about their corectness and the myths or the stories have been fabricated and woven around these important personalities. This literature more or less is full of descriptions of a particular deity, ceremonials in her honour descriptions of some parts of India as well as politics, science, iconography, warfare and so on.[9]

The Śākta Upa-Purāṇas

Though we find ample material pertaining to Devī-worship in the Major *Purāṇas* like *Markaṇḍeya Purāṇa, Vāmana Purāṇa, Varāha Purāṇa,Kūrma Purāṇa Śiva Purāṇa, Brahma Vaivarta Purāṇa,*[10] *and lastly Devi Bhāgavata* (not accepted by all as *Mahā Purāṇa*)—but it is only in the *Upa-purāṇas* that we find the complete works dedicated to the cult of *Śakti*. The *Upa-purāṇas* are related very often to the central goddess and sometimes to one or other of her principal forms such as *Dūrgā, Kālī, Chaṇḍī, Satī,* etc.[11] The three *Upa-Purāṇas,* viz. the *Devī Purāṇa, Kālikā Purāṇa,* and *Mahābhāgavata Purāṇa* are in printed form and deal with *Śakti* worship. We may agree with R.C. Hazra's view that all these three *Upa-Purāṇas*, must have been written in Bengal, rather its eastern part or Assam.[12] Now we will investigate the individual *Upa-Purāṇas*.

The Devī Purāṇa

It is one of the most important and the oldest *Upa-Purāṇa* dealing mainly with the exploits and worship of devi known as Vindhyavāsinī[13]. It gives us important information about the original nature of the goddess[14], about Yoga[15], and the method of its practice about *Śakta* iconography,[16] the *Śākta* vows and the worship[17]. It also furnishes information regarding the construction of towns and forts,[18] about the science of medicine,[19] about holy places alongwith the names of the countries and towns of historical value.[20]

The *Devī-Purāṇa*, consisted of 128 chapters, begins abruptly with an opening verse[21] without any introduction. The name of the reporter is unknown but he gives us information that *Vaśiṣtha* requested by the sages will recite the *Purāṇa*.[22] Vaśiṣtha divides the *Purāṇa* in four sections called *Pādas*.

1. The first *Pāda*, called as *Trailokya Vijaya* deals with the origin of Devī at the begining of creation.

2. The second *Pāda* known as *trailokyābhūdaya* deals with the story of *Indra* the killing of *Dundubhi*, *Ghora's* rise, Devī's descent on the *Vindhyas* and the numerous forms of Devi.

3. The third *Pāda* is named as *Sumbha-Niśumbha-Mathana*.

4. The fourth *Pāda*, not clearly named, deals with Andhak's fight; war between *Kārtikeya* and the demon *Tāraka*, origin of *Umā-Kālī* and residence of the Mothers in different regions for the good of children.

The present *Devī Purāṇa*, unfortunetely does not contain the whole of the original *Devī Purāṇa*,[23] as we can infer by the study of the contents of the *Purāṇa* as given in the first chapter and by the study of the whole text. In the present *Devī purāṇa*, we find only those topics which are said to be the topics of the second *Pada*.[24]

The *Devī Purāṇa* is certainly an old work though it has not been included in any of the comparatively early lists of the eighteen *Purāṇas* and the *Upa-purāṇas* in the different *Purāṇic* and non *Purāṇic* works.[25] As a large number of *Nibandhakāras*, both early and late, has quoted from this *Purāṇa*, the *Purāṇa* is to be placed not later than about 600 A.D.[26] In this *purāṇa* we also find references showing the prevalence of the worship of *Brahmā*, the deity, thrown into the background towards the beginning of the 7th century A.D.[27] Hence it can be said that the *Devī Purāṇa*, as we have it now, comes down from the 6th century A.D. and most probably from its latter half.[28]

About the place of origin of this *Purāṇa* we can better quote:[29] 'the *Devī Purāṇa* is an East Indian work written in Bengal, near about *Tāmluk* where situated a famous temple of the goddess *Vindhyavāsinī*.'[30]

The language is mainly *Prākṛt* and *Apabhraṁsa* which forms the basis of the *Un-pāniṇian* Sanskrit of this *Purāṇa*, and thus it occupies a unique position in the *Purāṇa* literature from the linguistic point of view.[31] It is said that this *Un-pāniṇian* language is not mainly due to the influence of *Mahāyana* Buddhist hybrid Sanskrit found in *Mahāvastu* etc. but it is based on the language of the *Pauṣkara Saṁhitā*.[32] In spite of its *Tāntric* elements, the *Devī Purāṇa* attained a great prominance as an authoritative work. It was so much popular that some enthusiastic *Śākṭas* thought it to be the original *Bhāgavata Purāṇa*, on account of its dealing with the glory, exploits and method of worship of Bhagavatī Dūrga.[33]

The Kālikā Purāṇa

The study of the *Kālikā Purāṇa*, discloses that the *Śākta* cult in its various phases was a predominant religion in Assam during the medieval period.[34] According to the *Devī Purāṇa*, the *Devī* was worshipped in different forms in

Kāmākhyā and *Kāmarupa.*[35] The *Kālikā Purāṇa,* a religio-ritualistic work, was written probably in Assam sometime in the 10th century A.D.[36]

The present *Kālikā purāṇa* containing 93 chapters has in main, two parts; the earlier section gives in detail the various accounts of *Śiva* and his consort *Pārvatī,*[37] the stories of the birth of *Kāmadeva,* marriage of *Śiva,* sacrifice performed by *Dakṣa,* origin of the river *Siprā* marriage of *Aruṅdhati,* fight between *Varāha* and *Śarabha,* conquest and death of *Naraka* and finally the story of *Betāla-Bhairava* and their pilgrimage to *Kāmarupa.* The sections in the 2nd part give descriptions of the worship of various gods and goddesses, and the accounts of the creation of the sacred places-*Pīthas* by the fall of the different limbs of the body of the goddess *Satī.* It further incorporates a few chapters on the duties of the kings.[38]

As one of the most important *Purāṇa,* it is regarded as an authority by the *Nibandha-Kāras,* especially with regards to *Śakti*-worship.[39] It is very important from the point of view, that it deals in details with the rivers, mountains, flora and fauna as well as with the cultural and religious history of Ancient Assam,[40] called *Kāmarūpa.* It records the progress made in the state under the rulership of the king *Naraka,* who has migrated from *Mithilā*; as well as it also depicts the chaos prevailing in the state under the *Malechha*-rule. This *Purāṇa* also attempts to regularise and codify the religious duties what the *smṛitis* had left.[41] It prescribes the worship of Śakti in her manifold forms as *Girijā, Devī, BhadraKālī, Kālī, Mahāmāyā* and others. It also gives in detail the *Bali* ceremony and draws a list of the animals to be offered to *Devī.*[42]

The Mahā-Bhāgvata Purāṇa

It is an *Upa-Purāṇa* dealing with the praise of *Devī* and her worship.[43] It is different from *Vaiṣṇava Mahā*

Purāṇā called *Bhāgavata* or *Mahā-Bhāgavata*. It is mentioned only in the *Bṛahaddharma Purāṇa*,[44] as *Māhā Purāṇa*, and is a comparatively late work. It is very important and interesting for the study of Hindu religion and society in Bengal specially in its eastern part adjacent to *Kāmārūpa*.[45]

This *Purāṇa* opens with four *Mangala Ślokas*, containing the slautations to Devi, the *Ādyā Prakṛtī*. About the origin of this *Purāṇa*, the first chapter records a traditon that *Vyāsa* the author of the *Purāṇas*, was not satisfied mentally even after writing 'the eighteen *Purāṇas*', and went to the *Himālayas* for realising the true nature of *Devi*, by means of austerities, and enable himself to write a *Mahā-Purāṇa* dealing elaborately with the praise of *Bhagāvatī*. Being pleased, Devī appeared in person before *Vyāsa*, and revealed the *Purāṇa* named the *Mahābhāgavata Purāṇa*.

This *Purāṇa* advocats that *Kālī*, who is *Parama Brahman* as well as *Parā Prakṛit*, is the wife and *Śakti* of *Śiva*.[46] Though it is mainly a *Śākta* work, but it praises *Śiva* worship also in strong words. It deals mainly with the praise of Devī, her incarnations to desteroy the demons, their exploits, praise of *Kāmarūpa*, and fifty one *Peeṭhas* of Devī.

It was written sometimes during the tenth or 11th cenuary A.D., either in *Kāmarūpa* or in that part of Bengal which was very near to it.[47] This *Purāṇa* was highly popular work[48] and was studied widely as an authoritative Purāṇa a few centuries ago.

A study of the *Purāṇa* shows that the author of this work lived in a society in which the sects like *Śaivas*, *Śāktas*[49] and *Vaiṣṇavas* were flourishing and was seriously influenced by Tantricism. People at that time studied the Agamas and followed *Tantric* manners, customs and methods of worship.[50] Even in their conceptions of the forms of the deities, they were guided by the *Tantras*.[51] So the author of the *Mahābhāgavat* praised *Varṇa śrama Dharma* and tried to bring about a compromise between the two systems.[52] Lastly *Mahā-Bhāgavata* advocates *Śaiva* tendency of *Śaktism* though it also follow in establishing the oneness of the gods.[53]

Concept of Śakti in Devī Purāṇa

The *Devī Purāṇa* is a great authority on *Śakti* worship and consequently is a work of extensive use. In this *purāṇa* or *Upa-purāṇa* Devi appears mainly as a war-goddess.[54] She is *Ādyā Śakti* and is not different from *Śiva Devī*.[55] She is named as *Chāmuṇḍa* and saved the life of *Viṣṇu*, in times of yore from the rage of *Kālāgni Rudra*. *Chāmuṇḍa* is said to be the powerful *śakti*, *i.e.* able to create protect and destroy the universe.[56]

In this *Purāṇa*, *Chāmuṇḍa* is told to be the burning flame of the fire of time, and is able to pacify the earthly fire.[57] she is said of the black complexion, besmeared with *Sindūra*, emitting the white rays of lusture she is the Controller of the gods like *Brahmā*, *Viṣṇu* and *Śiva*; as well as the creator and ruler of the gods, demons, human beings and semi-divine beings, as well as birds, animals and inanimate beings.[58]

Chāmuṇḍa is said to be living in the cemetry grounds.[59] and is ascribed with the work of destruction of the enemies. She is also said to be the fulfiller of all the desires.[60] At the same time she provides with religious merits, final salvation and wordly enjoyments.[61] She is the prime force belonging to Śiva, Viṣṇu and other gods. She is the great goddess, said to be having varied forms.[62] She is eternal pervading in all the beings, and progenitor of all the desires including the mental thinking.[63]

Nārada eulogises Devī,[64] who, though originating from Rudra; creates and protects *Brahmā*, *Viṣṇu*, *Śiva* and is known under different names viz.,

Durgā,
Sākambharī,
Gaurī,
Vindhya Vāsinī Kātyāyni Kauśiki,
Kaiṭabheśwarī,
Mahā Devī,
Mahābhogā. Maha Śveta,
Maheswarī,
Tridaśavandinī,
Iśānī,
Bhavīnī,
Bhūtabhavānī,
Jyeṣṭhā,
Śaṣṭhi,
Brahmavādinī,
Aparṇā,
Kapālā,
Suvarṇā,
Gāyatrī,
Sāvitrī. Ekapāṭalā,
Triśūlini,
Trinayanā,
Tripadā,
Trigunātmikā,
Śraddhā,
Swāhā,
Lakṣmi,
Sarvajñā,
Sarvatobhadrā,
Sarvotokṣi Śiromukhā,
Sarvabhutādi-madhyāntā,
Sarvalokeśwarī,
Mānavī,
Yādavi,
Yoganidrā,
Vaisnāvi,
Arupā,
Bahūrūpā,
Surūpā,
Kāma rūpinī. Śailrājasutā,
Sādhavi,
Mother of Skanda,
sister of Kṛṣṇa,
Sṛuiti,
Smṛtī,
Kālarātrī,
Mahārātrī,
Bhadrakālī,
Kapālinī,
Chamuṇḍa,
Chandrikā,
Chaṇḍi,
Chaṅḍa-muṅḍa-Vināśinī,
Rudrāṇī,
Pārvatī,
Indrāṇī. better half of *Śiva,*
Dākṣayanī,
Nārī,
Nārāyāṇī,
Śumbha-Niśumbha-Damanī
Mahisāsuraghātini, having one thousand eyes,
Dhīrā,
Revatī,
Siṃhavāhinī,
Viśvavatī,
Vīryavatī,
Vedamātā,
Sararwātī,
Māyāvatī,
Bhogāvatī,
Satī,
Satyavatī,

performer of all the activities, fulfiller of the desires, affectionate to the devotees and to the helpless persons, *Bhīmā, Ugrā, Dhūmrā, Ambikā, Trayambaka-priyā, Jayā, Vijayā, Ajitā, Aparājitā,* dweller in the heart and *Pāpanāśinī* and soon. Out of these 108 names of the goddess, 45 are her names identifying the goddess with other goddesses and rests and her appelations denoting her nature and her heroic deeds.

Sarvarūpā Devī

Devī is to be worshipped at *Kapota Tīrtha* which is compared in sanctity with *Māyāpurī* and *Kasī.* Here Devī is said *Sarvarupā* All the gods, human-beings and *Hara, Viṣṇu,* etc. are said to be the divine forms of Dev*ī.* She is the mother called also *Śivā a*s well as *Nārāyanī.*[65] She as *Prākṛiti* is composed of three guṇas (*Sattva, Rajas,* and *Tamas*), and is having three forms *Māhākālī, Mahā Lakṣmi* and *Mahā Saraswatī*), and having *Triśūla* in her hand. She is said to be surrounded by the ,Mothers.[66] In the image of gold or silver or in *Triśūlā,* she should be worshipped with due devotion.

Goddess from the lustre

All the *Śākta Purāṇas* agree that the goddess was the name of the united forces of the gods. For that purpose these *Purāṇas* have originated a theory that she was formed of the lustre (*Tejas*) of all the gods.[67] The *Devī Purāṇa* Says that when *Śiva* was worried about the demons, one *Tejas* appeared before him and changed into a goddess. This very goddess was called *Śakti, Kālī* or *Katāyanī.*[68] This *Tejas* was belonging to *Śiva* who desired to kill the demons.[69] This account with some variations, is found first of all, in the *Sapta Śatī* of the *Mārkaṇḍeya Purāṇa.*[70] Here it is said that *Viṣṇu* initiated the move by parting his lustre. In *Devī Bhāgavata Purāṇa* also, we find the same account, but here it is added that seeing the lustre, gods being frightened asked her and then they saw a very beautiful demsal, *i.e.* Devī-standing before them. It seems that author tried to avoid the fearful sight of Devī, called *Bhuvaneśwarī.*[71] The same *Purāṇa* again creates the goddess Umā *Haimavati* from the Tejas.[72]

In *Devī Purāṇa* we find Devī in all pervading form and is honoured by everyone. Even the gods like *Brahmā, Viṣṇu* and *Śiva* praise and worship her. Here we see that Śiva eulogised *Devī* with *Mahādaṇḍaka* hymn, in which he called Her, *Śiva* V*aktrodbhavā,*[73] *Pramatha-Laksha-vṛtā, Hema varnā, Smasānapriyā, Kamari Sānkhya-Yogodbhvā Bhadrakālī, Mahākalī and Mahāvṛkshaghaṇṭa-ravodgiti-karnotsavā.* She is also identified with *Brāhmī,* Kaumari, Mahendri Māheśrarī Vaisnavi *Varāhi, Sarasvatī,*[74] and other female deties. She is said to dwell in *Hemakūta, Mahendra, Himādri, Vindhya, sahya,* and *Śrigiri* mountains as well as on the mountain tops and in tthe caves.[75]

The Chapter 36 describes Devī as the cause of the creation, preservation and destruction of the world.[76] She is pervaded in whole of the universe. she is *Nāda-Vindu-rūpṇī* [77] having form of Mantras,[78] *Śiva Śakti Swarūpiṇi,*[79] *Parā* and *Aparā* and having *Virat* form.[80] She is the destroyer of the enemies, effort in times of war,[81] and is identified with *Kātyāyanī; Sūlinī Durgā, Gaurī* [82] and *Chaṇḍī* she is of the benign nature bestowing peace, happiness and fearlessness to the devotees.[83]

Unity of goddess and her pervasiveness

She is alone without a second,[84] but due to ignorance, people think her in many ways, and give examples. Some people think that *Rudra* is the cause of the world, others think about *Viṣṇu* and *Brahmā* but forget that all of them are, but the form of *Devi*[85] who is manifested in many ways due to three *guṇas*. As *sphaṭika Maṇi* being one, is represented variously due to different colours, similary goddess is one. Examples given are of the clouds rain water, wind, odour, fire to understand Devī's oneness.[86] This visible world is a manifestation of Devī and she pervades it. She is manifested in the form of varied names and bodies. she is said to be praised with Bhakti.[87]

Devī is known under different names. viz. *Nārāyaṇi Tārā, Śvetā, Mahāśvetā, Śivā, Gaurī, Carcikā, Vimalā, Umā* and *Ambikā.*[88] She is to be worshipped by the names *Charchickā Chāmuṇḍā, Nandā* on a sword, dagger , footwear, picture, a book flag, bow, image or alter.[89]

Devī is said to be giving the worldly thing, to her devotees. she is said in her benign forms mainly to be the curer of the diseases specially of the children.[90] The various diseases caused by the irregularity of *Vāta, Pitta,* and *Kapha,* and accidental fractures, even the cases of poisoning, snake biting, and the wounds caused by nails and teeth all these are cured by her. She can relieve the person from the diseases caused by even bad stars, *Bhūtas* and *Piśachas,* etc. The person suffering mentally or physically due to the crimes or sins, may be made free by the goddess. Even the murderers may feel mentally relaxed by remembering our goddess.

In a passage in *Devī Purāṇa* there is a very strange statement by *Śiva* that he is the father of Devī and at the same time Devī is his mother.[91] She is his sister as well as his wife. Devī as a sister of Śiva was called only in the *Vedic* period otherwise she is said to be the sister of Vāsudeva and wife of *Śiva* only.[92]

Kanakeśwarī

Devi *Kanakeśwarī* lives in a city constructed and decorated very beautifully, and the building is also palatial one. She comes to the place in a *Vimāna*[93] and is worshipped in the following manner

1. Image of Devi, made of *candrakāntamaṇi* is wor-

shipped in every house[94] by the ladies, for the sake of a husband.

2. Idol made of *Muktā* is worrshipped in the *Puri* of *Sunanda*[95] Devi.

3. Idol of *Sphatika* is worshipped by the ladies for the good of their husband,[96] in their own houses.

Note. In times of *pralaya,* only two goddesses remain while others are absorbed in the goddess.[97]

Goddess *Jayā* has been praised by *Indra* as a protector of the persons who are supportless. She proptects all the *devas* headed by *Brahmā.*[98] she is the deity meditated upon through *Yoga*, as the ultimate realty.[99] She is worshipped in the sacrifice with the recitation of the *Mantras* by the followers of the *Yoga* system and the *Sānkhya* philosophy.[100] She is without beginning and end and is respected even by the God *Śiva*. She is presiding in everyone.[101] She is told to be born from the body of *Śiva,*[102] as well as she is the mother of *Śiva, Viṣṇu* and *Brahmā*. and she invites *Rudra* to destroy the world.

SARVAMAṄGALĀ

The goddess *Sarvamangalā*, also called *Mangalarūpinī* is said to be the destroyer of demon *Rūru.*[103] she is again identified with that *Para Brahma*[104] as well as with the different goddesses of Hindu Pantheon viz. *Bhairavī, Durgā, Kanyā, Kapāli, Kālī*, etc.[105]

She is worshipped in the following manner:

1. Worship in the month of *Āśvin or Māgh* or *Chaitra* or *Śrāvana*, from dark 8th day to bright 9th, *i.e.* for 16 days.[106]
2. Observing the fast on the previous and on the *Pūjā* day.[107]
3. Feeding of the Brahmins, Gurus and their worship.[108]
4. Worship of girls and offering of food to them.[109]

5. Worship of Devi with different names.[110]
6. Recitation of the names of Devī.[111]
7. Homa is performed wih Devī Mantras.[112]
8. Offering of meat in the Balidāna ceremony.[113]
9. Arrangements of the cultural programmes,[114] like dancing and musical concerts in the night.
10. Donations according to one's means to Brahmins, teachers and girls.[115]
11. *Rathayātrā Mahotsava* of *Devī.*[116]
12. Mental devotion to *Devī.*,[117] called *Parā Bhakti.*

MANGALĀDEVĪ

Devī Purāṇa says that *Mangalā Devī* may be installed among the group of Mothers (*Mātṛkās*). On the southern side should be installed the goddesses *Brāhmī,* etc. and on the Northern side should be placed the goddess *Vaiṣṇavi* and so on.[118]

VINDHYAVĀSINĪ

Devī Purāṇa speaks that the gooddess *Vindhyavāsinī* resides constantly in *Vindhya* mountain. She manifested herself on the earth to kill demon *Ghora*. She is called *Nandā devī* when resides in the *Himālayas*. If worshipped with *Mantra, Dravya, Kriyā and Dhyāna,* she fulfills all the desires of the devotees.[119] If worshipped or remembered by the children, ladies or disabled persons, she becomes pleased easily.

The *Devī Vindhyavāsinī* is a manifestation of the goddess specially treated in *Devi Purāṇa*. The *Purāṇa* deals mainly with the exploits and worship of Devī (the great goddess) who incarnated herself on the *Vindhyas*, as a maiden mounted on a lion and became known as *Vindhyavāsinī.*[120] It is said that to kill the demons *Vajra daṇḍa* and *Kāla*, who were enjoying the supremacy over the three world, and on the request of Brahmā, *Viṣṇu* and *Śiva*, the goddess incarnated on the *Vindhyas* with a lion as her *Vāhana* and with *Brahmā, Viṣṇu* and *Śiva* as her servants and with so many unmarried female deities as her attendants.[121] The Sage *Nārada* went to demon *Vajra daṇḍa* to report about the young damsel (Devī), of divine beauty and residing in the *Vindhyas*. After knowing the fact the latter, with the intention of enjoying a mountain girl, marched with his army in an auspicious moment but exprienced various kinds of bad omens including the sight of a person wearing red clothes.[122]

The demon *Ghora* saw *Devī* on the *Vindhya* mountain and desired having her. He sent his commandor *Durmukha* in the month of *Āśvina* and he was killed by the goddess *Vijayā*.[123] Then a demon named *Kāla* was sent to arrest *Durgā*,[124] and Goddess *Jayā* came to fight with the army of the *asuras* and ultimately after a tough fight *Kāla* was sent to *Yamapuri* by Devi.[125]

Śiva-Umā

There is a *Stotra* in *Devī Purāṇa*, Where Devi is said to be the better half of *Siva*.[126] In this *Stotra* she is praised along with *Śiva*. In one verse some of the epithets are of *Śiva* and some of Devī. World is said to be consisted of *Śiva* and *Śakti*[127] only.She is *Sarvamanglā*, cause of all the causes, Lord of all, controller of all the worlds, and propounder of all the Yoga schools. She is *Rudrī* and *Mahāraudri*, lord of *Raudra*, respected by all the gods and demons, and knowledge Herself. She is incharge of the *Gaṇas*, having limitless power *Chaṇḍā, Durgā ,Prachaṇḍā, Chandśwari*,and *Ugrasanchārī*. She is the performer of difficult vows, full of anger, anger incarnate for the destruction of demon, *Nārāyanī, Kaumāri, Jayā, Vijaya, Nityā, Ajitā, Aparājitā* and success in *tapa* for the devotess. Divine mother is adorned with vowels and consonents. (letters), *Mahāmāyā*, Mother of the *Vedas*, and praised by the *Vedas* and full of Supreme knowledge. she is *Brahmāṇī*, riding on at swan, and pervaded in the sky, neither regions, in heaven, giver of salvation, and incarnate in all the beings. She is *Kriyā*,

Śaktī, Kālā, Jñāna and Bhakti. She shares all these qualities with *Śiva*. Both being pleased with gods managed to kill the demon Ruru.[128]

Kṣemankarī

She is identified with primeval force[129] and appears before the gods when requested by them, to kill demon *Subala* who had troubled the gods. She is having terrible form,[130] appearing as an old lady, emaciated, whose veins are visible, body without flesh, eyes in pits, ears half decorated, worried, with opened mouth, trempling, frightening the world, and equipped with hundreds of weapons. She surrounded with eight *Vidyās*, is situated in the middle of the

Kraunch Dwīpa

She always protects gods, therefore is called *Kṣemankarī*.[131] She being aged, is especially worshipped in *Pitṛpakṣa* with offerings of *Bali*, meat, fish, wine, gold, according to the ways either of *Kulamārga*,or *Vāma* and *Dakshiṇa* schools of wordship.[132]

Nandā Devī

God *Śiva* praises the Himālaya saying that there are four Tīrthas on the *Himālayas*, one of them being the *Nandā* Tirtha, where all the gods reside.[133] This is the most sacred in the world,[134] as the goddess called Nandā reside her.[135] Months of *Bhādrapada*, *Āṣādha*, *Śrāvaṇa* are said the best months for the pilgrimage to Nandā Tīrtha.[136] *Nandāpuri* is a very good place well-equipped with all the luxuries habitated by the gods and divine damsels waiting for Devī.[137] It can be compared with the *Maṇidvipa* described in the Devī *Bhāgavata Purāṇa*.

Ruru episode

The *Purāṇa* mentions war betweeen the goddess and

the demon *Ruru,* a new name in the *Śākta* mythology. From the mouth of peacock of Kartikeya, is originated the demon *Ruru*. By worshipping *Brahmā* he obtained a boon not to be killed by anyone else except the goddess. Gods being troubled by him went to *Viṣṇu* for the sake of protection. *Viṣṇu* praised *Śiva* and *Śakti* for the destruction of *Ruru*, he fought with *Śiva* and *Śiva* though not defeated but was not able to overpower the demon *Ruru*. The *Brahmā* came to help *Śiva* in this fight.

Brahmāṇī

The *Purāṇa* states that *Brahmā* changed His form as *Brahmāṇī* [138] to help *Śiva* in the fight against the demon *Ruru*. From the lustre of *Brahmā* there arose a goddess having a form of *Brahmāṇī* full of *Tejas*,[139] having *Kamaṇḍlu*, bow, weapon in her hands, and riding on a chariot yoked by swans. She was destroying the army of the demons like anything.

Durgā

Devī Purāṇa shows that *Durgā* was included in Indian pantheon by this time. There is an injunction in the *Purāṇa* to worship *Durgā* along with *Gaṇeśa Navagraha* and *Śiva*, while constructing a palace and a city.[140] One of the derivations of the name *Durgā* is the presiding deity of *Durgā*, the fort.[141] That is why we find the various names of *Durgā—as Giri Durgā*, *Vana Durgā* etc. which show some relation with the varieties of *Durgas* namely *Giri Durga* or *Vana Durga*.

In *Devī Purāṇa* there are instuctions regarding the construction of gates (Gopura), at both the sides of these should be installed the images of Devī *Mahisa Mardiṇī*. The gates should also be named after the different names of *Devī*.[142] At the time of the laying down the foundation of the fort, *Bāli* ceremony[143] is to be performed. *Śakti* is having so many forms. Poet says that sometimes she is having ten forms , or hundreds of forms, or innumerable incarnations, and still she is one. She is considered as an authority in all the *Vedas* and the *Vedanta.*[144]

Many times the author wants to identify the goddess *Kālī* with the god *Kāla.*[145] The destructive aspects of *Kāla* or *Rudra* (*Kālāgni-rudra*) is also ascribed to the Goddess.[146] The *Śakti* or Kālī is said to be the source of the three deities—*Brahmā, Viṣṇu* and *Śiva.* Though she is *Nirguṇā* or un-manifested, she manifests herself in the world in the form of deities.[147] She associates herself with the gods as their consorts and sometimes remains as their creator or instigater, and is called both *Deva Patnī* and *Deva Mātā.*[148]

Devī Purāṇa is the Bible of Brahmanical Śaktism.[149] It mentions *Tantras* and the *Agamas* frequently and also the *Bauddhas,* who worship the divine mothers in their own ways. It distinguishes between right-hand and left hand worshippers. The latter were to be found in *Rādhā* and *Varendra* (in Bengal), *Kāmarūpa* and *Kāmākhyā* in Assam; Bhoṭṭa *Deśa* (Tibet) etc. Some of the places it mentions indicate that the *Purāṇa* was written most probably in Bengal.

It is note worthy that this *Purāṇa* permits the *Pukvasas, Chaṇḍālas* and other outcaste group to perform the rituals and sacrifices to the goddess and even prefers for her worship a virtuous *Śudra* to a worthless member of one of the higher castes.[150] This agrees with the statement in the *Harivaṁśa Purāṇa*, that *Durgā* was worshipped by such aboriginal peoples as the *Śabaras, Barbara* and *Pulindas* who were addicted to meat and wine. The worship of a married woman and of the virgin girls, as manifestations of Devi, is also prescribe in this *Purāṇa.*[151]

The *Purāṇa* regards the *Vedas* as the highest authoriy and mentions the four Vedas. It has prescribed the *Gayatrī Mantra* for *Japa* and various other *Vedic Mantras* have been utilised in the performance of Homa.[152] All this shows a great influence of the Vedas upon it.[153] On the other hand it also exhibits the influence of the *Tantras*.[154] The *purāṇa* recognises the *Tantras* as an authority and mentions *Tantras* and the *Āgamās* on several occasion even by their names.[155] The form of worship is mainly *Tantric* and requires the use of the *Tantric Mantras, Nyāsas* and *Mudrās*.[156] It goes to the extant of prescribing use of wine and meat for the devotees.[157] We can only conclude that this *Purāṇa* is infused with *Tantric* influence from the beginning to end.

The *Purāṇa* is very important as it gives us important information about the different incarnations of Devī and her original nature as well as relationship with *Śiva* and other gods. All the names of the demons, who fought against Devi, occuring in this *Purāṇa* are new one. Though the *Purāṇa* has stressed more the ritualistic side of the *Śakta* cult, but it also describes various feats of Devī *Vindhyavāsinī* and her manifestations as well as places dear to her.

Form of Śakti in the Kālikā Purāṇa

The *Kālikā Purāṇa* is one of the most important works on *Śakti*-worship.[158] It is informed in the *Purāṇa* itself that the sage *Mārkaṇḍeya*,[159] requested by the sage *Kamaṭha* and others, recited this *Purāṇa*. The *Purāṇa* deals in its earlier sections with the following topics- How *Satī* was born of *Dakṣa*, how she had fascinated *Śiva*, and how she was reborn in the *Himalāyas*[160] and ultimately was married to *Śiva*. Mainly this *Purāṇa* deals with exploits and worship of *Kali* who is primarily the *Yaganidrā and Māyā of Viṣṇu,*[161] but later on became the wife of *Śiva* as the dark-complexioned *Śati* or *Kālī*, for the goods of the world.[162]

Dakṣa as a Devotee of Ambikā

First time in this *Purāṇa* we find *Dakṣa Prājapati* to celebrate the worship of Devī (*Viṣṇumāyā*) and performing

Havana for her so that she may be born in this house as his daughter.[163] She accepted the request on the condition that he would not neglect Her in any circumstances. First time we see that hatred towards the Rudra and *Pārvatī* (Non-āryan- deities) was removed and they were accepted in the Hindu pantheon.

The *Mahābhāgvata Purāṇa* also says that *Dakṣa* worshipped her so that she may be born as his daughter. The *Purāṇa* also says that even *Himavāna* and *Menā* performed *Tapa*, and were rewarded by her birth as their daughter.[164]

Yoganidrā

Yogindrā is also called *Viṣṇu-māyā*, *Mahāmāyā* and *Yoga māyā* and is described as the cause of creation, preservation and destruction.[165] In the *Kālikā-Purāṇa* she is said to have taken the form of *Kālikā*,[166] mounting on a lion, having dark complexion, four hands, a beautiful face and red eyes, having a sword and a blue lotus in the two of her hands and assuring boon and safety with the other two. In the *Mārkaṇḍeya Purāṇa* she is identified with *Mahāmāyā*, who deludes the whole world. She is able to lead towards the delusion even the minds of the learned persons.[167] She is supreme eternal knowledge being the cause of *Mokṣa*,[168] and is also the supreme power over all the gods. She is the power of *Viṣṇu* in *Devī Bhāgavata*[169] P. and is called *Purāṇa Prakṛit*, having preserved in her own body, the seed of creation.[170]

Parā Śaktī or Parā Brahman

The *Kālikā Purāṇa* presents *Devī* as *Parā Śakti*,[171] manifesting herself for the betterment of the world and the protection of the gods, from the terror of the demons. She is identified with *Brahman* and is called the power of each and every being. She illuminates the world with her own lustre and is residing in the heart of everybody.[172] She is *Vidyā* and *Avidyā* both, thus the cause of release and bondage both. She is the creation and the creator both. Here the author is talking in the terms of Upniṣads saying that she is without body or form and also with form. She is the biggest as well as the subtlest, the purest and the darkest. She alone preserves, creates and dissolves the world. She is the knowledge and the knower herself.[173] She is of the nature of bliss, knowledge and *Mantra*. She is *Mahāmāyā* as she deludes all the beings in the world. She is *Anantā* and *Śakti* or *Parā Śakti*. *Śakti* is ever-existing and gives her own *swaroop* to every devotee.[174] She is the *Mūla Prākṛtī* and still beyond the reach of our perception.[175] Here it is said that whatever important or powerful is there in the world, it only belongs to *Parā Śakti*.[176]

Viṣṇu Śakti

In the *Purāṇa*, Devi is assoicated with *Viṣṇu* though she is the wife of *Śiva*.[177] She was requested by Brahma to incarnate in the world as well as to marry *Śiva*.[178] She is also called *Kālī, Śaṅkarī* and *Rudrānī*, when born of *Dakṣa*,[179] and is Viṣṇu-priyā also. The *Purāṇa* distinguishes between the *Yoga-māyā, Mahā māyā,, Viṣṇu-māyā, Yoga-nidrā*, and last of all identifies them with Vaiṣṇavi.[180] Dakṣa seeing the goddess *Kālī*, praised her as *Lakshmī*.[181] Even the creation is ascribed to her.[182] As *Māyā* she eludes everyone and in the end she takes away that delusion.[183] For her worship also there are two methods; one is prescribed by *Vaiṣṇavi Tantra* and another by *Durgā Tantra*.[184]

Thus the *Purāṇa* exhibits an enormous *Vaiṣṇava* influence upon the cult of *Śakti*. It further shows that in its early hood the cult of *Śakti* either had no association or little association with *Śiva*. She was associated more with *Viṣṇu* and the worship was consisted of puritan type.

Marriage account of Śiva and Devī

First of all *Śiva* was married to *Satī*—the daughter of *Dakṣa*.[185] Here unlike the other *Purāṇas* it is said that when *Dakṣa* insulted *Śiva* and *Satī*, not inviting them in the sacrifice, *Satī* burnt herself on the *Kailāśa* itself. She did not go to the sacrificial ground, *i.e.* her fathers house.[186] *Śiva* taking her dead body on his shoulders moved, hither and thither, in a frantic way and the gods with the help of *Śani* made the pieces of that dead body.[187] This is the story of the creation of *Śakti-Pīṭhas*. Later on she was born as *Pārvatī* in the house of *Himavān*.[188] She even was of black colour and was called *Kālī* by her father.[189] She performed *Tapa* to obtain *Śiva* as her husband.[190] She was named as *Umā* by her Mother. The later portion of the story of the marriage of Śiva and Pārvatī is similar to the story described in *Kumāra* sambhava of *Kālidāsa*. The marriage was arranged by *Nārada* and seven sages—(Here we find the condemnation of *Śiva* which shows that there was a section of the people not worshipping him and his consort). Ultimately *Kālī* was married to *Śiva*.[191] They enjoyed for long living on the Mount *Kailāśa* and gave birth to *Skanda* and *Gaṇeśa*. The author says that *Kālī* is very dear to *Śiva*, and she is half of *Śiva's* body. He gives a new name to both these as *Ardhanāriśvara*.[192]

Mahāmāyā

She is the presiding goddess of the *Kālikā Purāṇa*.[193] She is the universal Mother called *Ambikā*. She is the *Mūla Mūrtī* and all other goddesses are only her different manifestions. She is also known by the names of *Mahisāsura-mardinī*; *Durgā; Kāmeśwari*, and *Bhadra Kāli*. She is a benevolent goddess, but is also called *Caṇḍikā*.[194] The *Purāṇa* describes her as the most beautiful lady in the world, wearing the golden ornaments and having fair complexion, decked with three eyes and four hands, having the weapon and *Siddha Sūtra* in her right hands and *varada* and *Abhaya* poses in her left hands.[195] She is also said to be having 18 hands. She is lustress like the ten million suns, and is very young. Her *Gāyātrī* is:—

ओं महामायायै विद्महे त्वां चण्डिकाख्यां धीमहि। धियो या नः प्रचोदयात्।[196]

She is worshipped with flowers, fragrants, lamp, and all luxurious thing along with other goddesses like *Koteśwarī, Bhuvaneśwarī, Kāmākhyā, Mātangī and Lalitā* etc.[197] Balidana,meaning the offering of meat of the animals to the goddess is prescribed here in detail.[198] Mahāmāyā is also Kāmākhyā, residing in Kāmarūpa.[199]

There are so many manifestations of *Devī*. The *Kālikā Purāṇa* also gives various names in the following order:

1. *Daśabhujā*—having ten arms, is called *Durgā*.[200]
2. *Aṣṭādaśabhujā*—eighteen handed form is called *Ambikā* who was worshipped by *Rāma* to kill *Rāvaṇa*. she is also clled *Vaiṣṇavi*, *Mahāmāyā*[201] and *Ugra Chandā*.[202]
3. *Ṣoḍasa Bhujā,—Sixteen handed goddess is called Bhadra Kālī*.[203]
4. *Daśabhujā*—having ten arms. She is called *Kātyāyanī*, formed out of the lustre of the gods and killed *Mahiṣāsura*.[204]

TĀRA OR CHĀMUṆḌĀ

Another form of *Māhāmāyā* is *Tārā* or *Chāmuṇḍā*. Her worship was once very popular in Assam and several images of *Chāmuṇḍa* also have been discovered in the province. The following description of *Tārā* or *Chāmuṇḍa* in our text shows a slight difference from the description given in the *Agni Puranā, Matsya Purāṇa* and *Viṣṇu Dharmottara Purāṇa*.[205]

"Her complexion is like the colour of a blue lotus. She has four arms and in her right hands, she holds *Khaṭv-āṅga* and *Chandrahāsa* and in her left hands *Charma* and *Pāśa*. She wears a tiger-skin and puts a garland of skulls on her neck. she is of a slender, long and terrible body with long teeth, having a protruding tongue, extended ears, vide face and red eyes, sunk in sockets. She is shown seated on Kabandha.[206]

Kauśikī

According to the *Kālikā Purāṇa*, the goddess *Kauśīki* sprang from the body of *Kālikā*.[207] She is an important deity next to Mahāmāya. The Devī *Māhāṭmaya* of the *Mārkaṇḍeya Purāṇa*, however states that the goddess *Kauśīki* was born from the body of the supremee goddess in a dazzling beautiful form.[208] The *Kālikā Purāṇa* also represents her in a very pleasing manner.[209]

Her locks are well-controlled in braids and she wears a down turned half moon on her forehead just above the sandal mark (*Tilaka*). Her checks are touched by bejewelled ear-rings; she is adorned with a crown and ornaments. She wears gold necklaces, set with jewells and garland of *Nāgas*. She is wearing a garland of fragrant lotuses,and a pair of gem-made armlets. Her tender arms are just like lotus stalks and she wears beautiful yallow garments. She has high breasts, covered with breast-caps, a slender waist and three folds in her belly. In her right hands are a *Śūla* a *vajra*, a *Bāna*, a sword and a *Śakti*; and in her left hands are a *Gadā*, a *Ghantā*, a *Cāpa*, a *charma* and a *conch*. She sits on a tiger skin placed on the back of a lion.

Dikkarvāsini

The *Kālikā Purāṇa* imported a new goddess named *Dikkarvāsinī* who was worshipped in the eastern regin of Assam. The goddess has two forms *Tikshṇa Kāntā* (dreadfully attractive) and *Lalitā Kāntā* (gracefully attractive).[210] Former is of black colour , pot-bellied and with one lock of matted hair so she is called *Ekjatā* also. Her six atteddants are *Chāmuṇḍa, Karālā, Subhagā, Bhiṣaṇā, Bhogā. Vikaṭā.* Her mode of worship in general, conforms to that of the goddess *Kāmākhyā*, although her most delectable offerings are consisted of strong spirituous liquor, human sacrifice, *Modaka* , flesh, curry, cocoa-nuts and sugar-cane.[211]

She is also called *Ugra Tārā.*[212] In this form her worship was once very popular and even today there is a temple at Gauhati known as *Ugratārā* temple where *Devī* is worshipped particularly in autumn with sacrifice of buffallows, goats etc. It is stated that *Ugratārā* was originally a benevolent goddess, but subsequently at the curse of the sage Vaṣistha she turned to be a malevolent one and came to be worshipped in the left hand way.[213]

The description of *Ugratārā in Kālikā Purāṇa* is different from that given in Tārā Tantra.[214]

LALITA KĀNTĀ

She is known more by her popular title Mangala Chaṇdī.[215] By this name she is worshipped even today in Assam and Bengal. She is to be meditated upon as follows:[216] She has two arms in *Varada* and *Abhaya* poses, her body is yellow, she sits on a red lotus, and is adorned with a bright crown and is attired in red silk. Her auspicious face is in a constant smile and her charming body is endowed with fresh youth. Mangla Chandī is to be meditated either on a picture, or image or a pot.[217] Further she is to be invoked according to the *Vaiṣaṇavavaite Tantras* and *Mantras* and with those offerings which are generally offered to the goddess *Mahāmāyā.*

UMĀ AND RUDRĀṆĪ

Umā is described having golden complexion and two arms. In her left hand she holds a blue lotus and in the right a white *Cāmara*. She stands on the right side of *Śiva*, resting her hand on him.[218] She is having eight attendant deities viz. *Jayā, Vijayā, Mātaṅgī, Lalitā, Narāyanī, Sāvitrī, Svadhā* and *Svāhā*. The goddes *Rudrāṇī* is depicted as having two arms and carrying lotus and *Chāmara* in each of them. She sits on a tiger skin placed ona lotus.[219]

TRIPURĀ BHAIRAVĪ

There are a large number of deities that were once

worshipped under various forms of goddess *Tripurā*. According to our text these are all different manifestations of the Great Goddess *Mahāmāyā.*[220] The goddess *Tripurā* first manifested herself as a virgin *Kumārī*, later on she divided herself into three forms of *Tripurā* aspect and further into *Gaurī Ramā*, *Bhāratī*, *Kālī*, *Chaṇḍikā*, *Durgā*, *Bhagavatī*, *Kātyāyanī*, *Parā*, *Lalitā*, and *Maharājnī.*[221] The three different forms of *Tripurā* as detailed in *Kālikā Purāṇa* are *Tripurā Bhairavī*. *Tripurā Balā*, and *Tripurā* Sundari.[222] The Purāṇa devotes several sections to the exposition of rites and ceremonies connected with the worship of the goddess *Tripurā* in her different manifestations. These discriptions differ largely from those in the *Tripurā Rahasya.*[223]

The *Bhairavī* form is one of the dominant manifestations of the goddess. She is to be worshipped in this form in the left hand ways.[224] Whatever is red dearer to *Tripurā Bhairavī*. Spirituous, liquors red flower, red clothing and vermillion please her the most.[225]

Kāmākhyā

She is the presiding deity of the *Kāmarūpa* as well as of the *Kālikā Purāṇa*. Though we find her name throughout the work, but in the latter half of the *Purāṇa* it is more common. When *Mahāmāyā* went to enjoy with *Śiva* at *Kāmarūpa* she was named as Kāmākhyā.[226] She resides on the *Nīla Kūṭa* mountain,[227] where the Śiva resides. She is called by the names of *Kāmākhyā*, *Tripurā*, *Kameśwarī*, *Kāmarūpā* and *Yoni-mandala.*[228] She is having five forms, and similarly five forms of Śiva are mentioned.[229] She is having fair colour, decked with ornaments, young age and is a lady of beauty.[230] Her *Mantra* is named as *Kāma Gāyatrī.*[231]

It is said that one should go to *Yoni-Piṭha* of *Kāmākhyā* and he will be relieved of the world.[232] The goddess is said as the Mother of the world and the creator of the universe.

THE VIRGIN GODDESS, TRIPURĀ

A considerable section of the *Kālikā-Purāṇa* has been devoted to the worship of the goddess *Tripurā*, a virgin goddess of beauty and sex, identified with *Pārvatī* and *Kāmākhyā*. The cult of the virgin worship (*Kanyā-Pūjan*) and of the sensual aspects of the Devi-worship seems to be derived from the cult of *Tripurā* recorded in the *Tripurā Rahasya*.[233] It is said in the *Yogini Tantra*,[234] that a *Sakta* devotee is to be enjoined to contem plate the mental image of a girl of sixteen, shinning like the newly rising sun. He has to become identical with *Tripurā Sundarī* and to think himself as a Devi or a woman.[235]

The *Tripurā Rahasya* furnishes certain details about the emergence of this goddess. She is the primordial. Energy embodied as *Mahādevī* (the great goddess). The whole world static and moving is her sport.[236] This Energy is to be contemplated as woman,[237] because the female form is considered both beautiful and pleasure giving, the very nature of consciousness and intelligence. So she is contemplated as a pleasing instrument of spiritual success.[238] The female figure manifested herself first as a virgin goddess and then she divided herself in several forms.

The goddess was called a virgin (*Kumārī*), because she was her own mistress and by virtue of her own independent status created the universe according to her desire.[239] Here by virgin we do not mean the present meaning of chaste, unspotted girl, but it means unwed, unmarried, and thus free from any body's control. The virgin Ishtar is frequently addressed as the prostitute. The sacred prostitutes in her temples were also called 'the holy virgins',.[240] (Devi Dāsis).

This beautiful goddess presiding over the circle of feminine triangles has been super-imposed upon, in her own complete self. In the *Kālikā Purāṇa* the *Tripurā* goddess is adored in three aspects as *Tripurā Bālā, Tripurā Sundarī*, and *Tripurā Bhairavī*.[241] *Tripurā Sundarī* has three poses and of these three, the middle pose is the focus of concentration. The form is that of a fair lady with all good bodily signs, and adorned with varied ornaments. She is of the splendour of the rising sun, full of freshness of the youth; seated on a counch of lotus flowers, with fully developed breasts, bejewelled with three fold wrinkles of flesh round the belly, slightly intoxicated with drink, pleasing to the eye and causing heavy undulations of passions in the world.[242] In the first and third poses she is depicted as naked.[243] *Tripurā Bālā* carries a flowery arrows and a noose.[244] *Tripurā Bhairavī* is red in colour and dressed in red garments. She is dazzling like a thousand suns with eyes rolling with intoxication of drink.[245] *Tripurābālā* may be worshipped according to the right hand or left hand rites, but *Tripurā-Bhairavī* must be worshipped according to the left[246]-hand method. *Bhairavī* is the most dominaing manifestation.[247]

This goddess has created nine *Śaktis* called *Kāmeśwari*, *Bhagamālinī* (bearing a garland of sex-organs), *Nitya Klinnā* (always moist, *Bhruṇatā* (pregnant) etc. and also nine yoginis.[248] The goddess herself dwells in the centre of nine triangles placed within one another, the whole being encompassed by one circle. This is called *Śrī Cakra,* situated within this circle she is called *Mahā-Tripurā Sundarī*.[249] She divides herself into nine parts and prisides over all the triangles, her several names being *Tripurā, Tripureśī Tripurā-Sundarī, Tripuravāsinī, Tripurā Śrī, Tripurā Mālinī. Tripurā Sīddhā, Tripurāmbikā and Mahā Tripurā Sundarī*.[250] Whosoever erects a *Śrīcakra* is entitled to get endless bliss.[251]

She dwells in her own real self in three places;[252] *Kāma Giri, Kāmākhyā hills;, Jullundhar* and *Ourangiri* near the sea. There are twelve manifestations of *Devī* dwelling in twelve places.[253]

1. Kāmākṣi in Kanchipura;
2. Kumārī (the virgin) in Kerala;
3. Sundarī (the beautiful)in Banga;

4. Guhyakeśwārī (the lady of the Guhyakas) in Nepal;
5. Bhrāmarī in Malaya;
6. Ambā in Anarta countary;
7. Mahālakshmi in Karavila;
8. Kālikā in Malaya;
9. Lalitā in Prayāga;
10. Vindhyavāsinī in the Vindhya hills;
11. Viśālakshī in Benaras;
12. Mangalvatī in Gayā.

THE NARAKA EPISODE

By the study of the *Naraka* episode,[254] D.R.Mankad suggests that the whole story points out towards the ancient chronological history of Assam[255] which is still to be traced. Main features are as follows:—

1. *Naraka* was the adopted son of *Janaka*, king of *Mithilā* and *Bhūmi*, a foster mother, possibly the follower of the *Śakta* religion.[256]
2. *Naraka* was a title of a dynasty just like *Janaka*, both meaning the same (नर + क; जन + क) and according to the book called *Hara Gauri Samvāda*, twenty four or twenty five kings in *Naraka* dynasty have ruled over Assam (*Kāmarūpa*).[257]
3. The first king in the *Kālikā Purāṇā* is called *Naraka* While it is the last king of the dynasty who is called *Narakāsura*, a man like *asura* but not belonging to asura dynasty.[258]
4. *Naraka* defeated the *Kirāt* king of *Kāmarūpa* and founded the rule of his dynasty there. It seems that as the Assam was habitated by the *Kirātas* etc. the cult of *Śakti* was prevalent there, which he followed to strenthen his position in the state, but at the same time he modified it by bringing the Brahmins, wellversed in the Vedas, from other states, and he was suceessful in his mission.[259]
5. The king *Naraka* established *Śaktism in Kāmarūpa* country and constructed a temple of *Kāmākhyā* on the top of *Nilāchal*. He was a devout follower of *Śakti* cult.[260]
6. The last king of the dynasty called as *Narakāsura*

began to disrespect Devi and introduced all singful acts in the state with the advice of the king *Banāsurā*, a worshipper of *Śiva*. He had also collected and imprisoned 16,000 beautiful girls.[261]

7. Kṛṣṇa on the request of the gods killed this *Narakāsura* and freed all those girls and he in stalled *Bhagadutta*, the son of grandson or *Narakasura* on throne.[262]

The study of the *Naraka* episode in the *Kālikā-Purāṇa* goes to point out that prevalent *Śakti* cult was of two types viz.

1. *Śakti-cult* was supported by Vaisnavism, as we see in the beginning of the *Purāṇa* that *Naraka* was offered a boon by *Viṣṇu* himself, rather he is called the son of *Viṣṇu.*[263]

This cult of *Śakti* sponsered by *Viṣṇu,* was of puritan style constituting the simple worship of the goddess with vegetarian offering. It was free from all *Tantric* miscrepancies like offering of meat, wine, *Bhairavī Cakra* and *Mudrā* etc.[264]

2. Cult of *Śakti* influenced by *Śaivism* as we see that as soon as *Narakāsura* the last king came in contact of *Śaivism* through *Bānāsura* is stated to commite all sinful acts. This indicates that the cult sponsored by *Śiva* was nonvegatarian cult with constituents of offering of *Bali,* commencements of Bhairavi-*Cakra, Mudrā, Yantras* and permiting to lead nonethical life.[265] In the end the king *Narakāsur* was killed by *Kṛṣṇa* to lighten the burden of the earth.

Thus we see a direct tussel between *Vaiṣṇavism* and *Śaivism* to influence the cult of *Śakti*. Originally, in this *Purāṇa Vaiṣṇavism* was overpowering the cult while in the later period it was Śaivism which influenced it so much so that in the end *Śaktism* was considered as part of *Śaivism.*[266]

KĀMARŪPA

What followed immediately the Naraka's death and

disappearance of the symbol of the goddess Kāmākhyā is not mentioned in the *Kālikā Purāṇa*, but the *Yoginī Tantra*, which takes a very lenient view of *Naraka's* conduct towards *Vaśiṣtha*, states that goddess *Kāmākhyā* was to suffer an eclipse for three hundred years of the *Kālī* era. There will be great sufferings of the people and none but a succession of tribal kings, the *Yavanas*, the *Kuvacas*,the *Saumāras* and the *Plavas* will rule over the country.[267]

Once *Kāmarūpa* became such a sacred place that all the people living there became entitled, by virtue of their residence in *Kāmārūpa*, to go to heaven after death. *Yama* felt greatly at this loss of control and lodged a complaint with *Brahmā* and subsequently the matter was reported to *Viṣṇu* as well as to *Śiva* who in return promised to help *Yama*. *Śiva* ordered the hosts and goddess *Ugra Tārā* to drive out all the twice born people from Assam. Goddess *Ugra Tārā* and *Aparājitā* expelled all the *Dvijas* and the people of the four-orders. *Vāsiṣtha* who was practising penances to *Śiva* on the *Sandhyachala* hill and who was forced to go out by the goddess *Ugra tārā*, pronounced a terrible curse on *Ugra tārā*, the hosts and *Siva* himself. He said, "you being a woman (*Vāmā)* are expelling me, so you will henceforth be worshipped only according to *Vāmā* rites. Your hosts roving aboutlike *Mlechhas* will henceforth be degraded to the rank of *Mlechhas*, and *Śiva* will receive only the worship by the *Mlechhas* being always covered over with ashes and carrying bones. This land of *Kāmarūpa* will be ruled over the *Mlechhas* and at the advent of *Viṣṇu* all the scriptures, will be rarities"[268] The curse of the saint had immediate effect and *Kāmarūpa* became shorn of *Vedic* rites, as the four orders of the people were driven out.[269]

Śaivism in some gross form assoicated with wine and flesh was the prevailing religon of the aboriginal *Kirāṭas*. The Aryanisad conquerors held this religion in disdain and placed it under a ban. At the same time to secure easy recognition by aboriginal people they brought to prominance another local-cult, the cult of the Mother goddess worshipped in the *Yoni* symbol as opposed to the cult of *Śiva* worshipped in the phallic symbol. This mother cult of *Kamākhyā* must have belonged to certain matriarchal tribes like the Khasis and the Garos. To win over their allegiance and support and to facilitate the propagation of *Āryan* ideas and customs, royal patronage was extended to this local cult of *Kāmākhyā.* The Mother Goddess in *Kāmarūpa* could very easily be brought into alignment with other forms of the Mother goddess like *Durgā, Kālī* etc. which had already been recognised and adored in the *Mahābhārata* and in the early *Purāṇas.* The *Saivas* scented a danger in this suppression of thier own cult and the escaltations of a rival cult. They secretly hatched a conspiracy not simply against the rival cult but against the prime instigators, i.e. the Vaiṣṅavite teachers and the Aryan twice-born. The king *Naraka* was won over from the Aryan ways and the symbol of the goddess *Kāmakhyā* was stolen, then *Naraka* was destroyed by his former supporters.[270]

Durgā, with her varied names had already established herself as a mighty goddess in thePaurāṇic Pantheon. In the *Harivaṁśa* she is also called *Nārāyaṅa—Priyā* (beloved of *Nārāyaṇa)* and *Vāsudevabhaginī* (sister of *Vāsudeva, Kṛṣṇa).* These epithets show her early associatin with *Viśṇu* and the Vaishnavite-cult. Commenting on this passage of the *Harivaṁśa,* Muir says—"The object of this passage seems to be to take *Durgā* and her worship under the protection and patronage of Viṣṇu.[271] This will explain why the worship of *Kāmākhyā* was encouraged and patronised by *Viṣṇu, Kāmākhya* being by his side against *Naraka.* In he early stages of her evolution, *Durgā* with her other manifestations had nothing to do with *Śiva.* Muir says,"It appears as if some contest had at one time existed between the votaries of *Mahādeva* and those of other deities and *Dakṣa Yajña* may be treated as the best example.[272]

Perhaps the temple of *Kāmākhyā,* on the west of Gauhati,

was associated with *Tantrik* Hinduism. The shrine represents, the *Yonī*, and is associated with the pre-*Āryan* king *Naraka*, who used to be the guardian of the shrine. According to the *Kālikā Purāṇa* the genital organ of *Satī* fell here on the *Nilāchala* hillock. She is called *Kāmākhyā* because she came there secretly to satisfy her amour (*Kāma)* with Śiva. Later religious history of Assam centres round this goddess; and other godesses are recognised as her varied manifestations.[273] The cult of virgin worship, and of the sexual aspect of the *Śakti*-worship seems to be derived from the cult of *Tripurā*, a virgin goddess of beauty and sex.[274]

The *Kālikā Purāṇa* is very important from the point of view of his history of *Śaktism*. It records so many stories to show the prevalence of the *Śakti*-cult. First time we find here the story about the origin or creation of the *Śakti Pīṭhas*. It is the only work in whole of the Puranic range which gives in detail the description as well as the prescription of *Paśu Bali* to the goddess. It alsos suggests the performance of *Mudras*, especially the *Yonī-mudrā*, very dear to the goddess. There are long dissertations on the topic of 16 *Upachāras* offered to *Devī*. In short the *Purāṇa* represents the ritualistic side of the *Śakti*-cult which was very popular in those days.

Śakti in the Mahā-bhāgavata Purāṇa

It is an interesting *Upa-Purāṇa* dealing with the praise of the Devi and her worship. The *Purāṇa* opens with the *Ślokas* saying *Devī* as *Ādyā Prākṛtī* and *Parī and Swarga-Apavarga*-pradā; she created the universe of her own accord, subjected herself to births, and had *Siva* as her husband.[275] In this *Purāṇa* the goddess is also calledas *'Tāraka Brahman*,[276] which in its form of *Durgā* stays at mountain Mandara.[277]

The *Purāṇa* advocates *Śaktism*. According to this *Purāṇa*, it is *Kālī* who is *Param Brahman* as well as *Parā Prakṛtī* (or *Mūla Prakṛtī*). Unlike the *Kālikā Purāṇa* and the *Bṛhaddharmā Purāṇa*, it conceives *Kālī* as the wife and *Śakti* of *Śiva*.[278] It identifies *Śiva* with *Puruṣa* and says that *Brahman* consists of *Śiva* and *Śakti*.[279] Thought *Sachidānnanda-Vigrahā, Śuddha-Jñānamayī* and *Arūpā, Kālī* as *Prākṛtī*, assumed for the sake of creation, the from of a young and beautiful lady seated on a lion and having a dark complexion, four hadns, red eyes, dishevelled hair, and the quarters as her clothes *(Digambarā)*.[280] She created a *Puruṣa* as an embodiment of the three Gunas and contaminated into him a wish for creation. From the three *Gunas*, (*viz. Sattva, Rajas* and *Tamas*), this *Purusa* were born *Brahmā, Viṣṇu*, and *Śiva* respectively. *Prakṛtī* on her part, divided herself into *Māyā, Vidyā* and *Paranā* and became *Satī, Gangā, Durgā, Sāvitrī, Lakśmī, Sarasvati* and others.[281]

Devī is said having a divine from.[282] She is *Sūkshma)* subtle nature and first born in the world.[283] Devi herself while revealing her nature to *Himālaya* says that 'I am ultimate power, mother of *Brahmā, Viṣṇu* and *Maheśa*, creator of the world, protector and destroyer also.[284] She is told to be *Brahman* of the *Vedanṭa*, comprised of bliss eternal, (*Nityānadmayī)* eternity incarnate, knowledge and bliss in bodily form.[285] She is always considered to be the mother of the wọrld, individual and of the deities or devotees, last of all is full of compassion.[286]

In *Devīgītā* she is all in the world[287] ranking with Brahman. Here in the *Mahābhāgavata* she is said to be having all the *Vibhūtis*[288] as it is said in the *Gītā* about *Kṛṣṇa*.[289] According to this *Purāṇa Śiva* and *Śakti* are not different. Both are but one, named as *Brahman*.[290] *She is* comprised of all the sacrifices (*Yajña*).[291] We can note here that *Bhakti*, just like *Vaiṣṇavism*, is the main tenate of *Śaktism* in this *Purāṇa*. *Bhaguvatī Gītā* of *Mahābhāgavatā Purāṇa* especially is a discourse on *Bhaktiyoga*, but the deity is said to be *Parāśakti*.[292]

Śakti and the power is said to be the great deluge of the world as well as she is the consciousness or knoweldge incarnate.[293] 'You are the last resort for the poor devotees suffering from worldly bondage and miseries.[294] Devī in her all the forms is considered to be the remover of poverty, she protects from all types of fears and punishes the wicked persons,[295] so that the gentle fellows may enjoy the world and attain the salvation.

Besides these philosophical speculations on Devī, the *Purāṇa* is very important for the cult of *Śakti* as it tries to show the relation of *Śaktism* with all the important personalities of Indian History, events and the great books named as epics. Though in the other *Purāṇas* also we find that *Rāma* worshipped *Durgā* and then killed *Rāvana* with her help, but the readers will be astonished to study in the *Mahabhāgavata,* that *Kṛṣṇa* also was on incarnarion of *Devī. Śiva* once requested *Devī* to be the husband and himself to be the wife, and this desire, as *Purāṇa-kāra* says, was fulfilled by the goddess in *Kṛṣṇa avātara.* She was herself born as *Kṛṇṣa* from *Devakī and Vāsudeva*, while *Siva* was born as *Rādhā,* being the beloved of *Śrīkṛṣṇa.*

In this *Purāṇa* and *Rāma* episode,[296] the *Kṛṣṇa* episode,[297] and the Pandavas battle against *Kauravas*[298] and *Indra-Vṛtra*[299] episode, all the main and important events of *Purāṇik* Mythology are related with the cult of *Śakti*. Thus the author tried to show the harmony between the *Śakti* or *Durgā,* with other sects of Hinduism viz. *Vaisṇavism* pertaining to both, *i.e.*, the *Rāma* and *Śrīkṛṣṇa* as well as Śaivism.[300]

Pāṇḍavas as devotees of Kālī

They are said to be the devout devotees of *Devī*[301] while Draupadi is said to be the partial incarnation of Devi[302], on whose insult the goddess was enraged and managed to kill the demons in the guise of the *Kauravas.* While going to *Matsya Desha*[303] they praised Her and in battlefield[304] they invoked Her. At every time of difficulty they tried to remember Her either in the form of *Kṛṣṇa* or in her *Kālī* form. While going to the forest they went to *Yonipeetha*[305], worshipped the goddess and asked her for kingdom, the Goddess was all the time by their side and protected them from every danger and made them to be successful in the great world war called *Mahābhārata*.

Incarnation of Devī as Śrikṛṣṇa

Once upon a time *Śiva* sitting on *Kailāsa* requested *Devī* to fulfil his only desire. The desire was that *Śiva* wanted himself to see in a woman form.[306] She agreed to it and promised to descend on earth in the form of *Śrikṛṣṇa*[307] to serve the following purpose

1. To enjoy with *Śiva* who incarnated n the form of *Rādhā.*[308]
2. To destroy the bad kings,[309] *i.e.* the incarnations of *Rākṣasas* killed by *Viṣṇu,* as she was requested by the Earth as well as by *Brahmā* to remove the burden from earth.

She counselled with *Viṣṇu* divided Herself in two[310]

1. A girl (later on *Vindhya-vāsinī)* born of Yaśodā.
2. *Srikṛṣṇa*[311] was born *Devākī* and was exchanged for some time to *Nanda's child.*

She was born as *Srīkṛṣṇa* and made *Devakī* to know Her real form *i.e. Kālī.*[312] She as *Śrīkṛṣṇa* managed to kill *Pūtanā, Bakāśura, Aghaśura,*[313] *Kaṇsa* and released his parents from *Kaṅsa's* prison. She enjoyed with *Rādhā* in *Rāsalīlā* (that means whole of the life of *Srikṛṣṇa* is being depicted, identifying him Kali).[314] Finally He helped the *Pāṇḍavas* to win the *Mahābhārata* was and destroyed and *Kaurvas.* A new thing is there that *Pāṇḍavas* went to *Svarga* alongwith *Srikṛṣṇa,*[315] as they did not want to live in the world without *Kṛṣṇa* (without Her grace). In this way *Kṛṣṇa* is shown to be the *Kālī* and the *Kālī* to be the *Kṛṣṇa; i.e.* both the deities and sects are shown as one.[316]

The Rāma Episode

The *Purāṇa* says that Rāvana was a devout devotee of the goddess and there was a temple of *Devī* in Lanka where he used to worship her daily. Being valorous due to her grace, he was invincible even by the gods.[317] Then Rama came on the earth, to destroy the Rāvaṇa, as he was turned to be a wicked person. Rāma also in his early childhood was initiated to *Devī Mantra.*[318] When Sītī, a manifestation of Devi, was taken away by Rāvana in Laṅkā, it was an incident which infuriated the goddess against him and she promised her full co-operation to Rāma against Rāvaṇa.[319] Rāma reaching Laṅka, her, and afterwards also with the advice of *Brahmā,* celebrated her worship. This ceremony was called *Akāla Bodhana,* meaning untimely worship, and thus was orginated the worship of Devi in the *Śarad Navaratra.* The Goddess appeared and offered a boon to Rāma that he will be able to kill Rāvaṇa.[320] Then in the four chapters, Devi and her abode as well her worship is described. Ultimately the Rāma was victorius over Rāvana and was very much greatful to *Śakti* or goddess by whose grace he succeeded in this extra-ordinary object, which earned him fame, kingdom and Sitā.[321] In this way it depicts the over-powering influence of Śaktism over Rāma, a *Vaiṣṇava* deity.

Indra and Brahmahayā

Indra when defeated by *Vṛtra,* went to *Dāhichi,* a seer, and asked him to help in the destruction of *Vṛtra. Dadhichi* after a long consideration left his body by *Yogāgni* so that the weapon may be made of his bones to kill *Vṛtra.*[322] Indra having done so ultimately killed his enemy and regained his kingdom. But as *Dadhichi* was destroyed, the *Brahma Hatyā* came to *Indra.* As and he wanted to remove it off he first of all went to *Gautama* to seek the means. *Gautama* told him have a look of *Mahākālī,*[323] and he will be clelansed of *Brahmā Haty.* But she was only to be seen by *Tapas* of many years, not possible for *Indra,* so he said that *Indra* should go to Her *Aboda,* about which he knew nothing. *Gautama* directed him to *Brahmā*, *Brahmā to Viṣṇu* and *to Śiva* to know Her *Loka. Śiva,* who has seen it by virtue of penance, went to *Kālī's Loka* along with *Brahmā, Viṣṇu* and *Indra.* While going there they saw so many *Brahmās, Viṣṇus* and universes and the luxury displayed there, they have fogot their aim and were abosorved in seeing that. Once some maid servant of Devī came to ask them and she reminded them of their main object.[324] Then they went to *Devīs* residence and through *Ganapatī* sent a message to devi, who sent him back to ask from which universe they are coming, as there were so many *Brahmāṇḍas* and *Devas.* But they were unable to answer. Anyhow Devī called them inside all except *Indra.*After few minutes *Kālī,* became *Antarhitā* [325] and it was after the *Stuti* (eūgy) by *Brahmā* and *Śiva* that she appeared again to bless them. *Śiva* then asked for the entry of *Indra* into her palace. She said that his sins are removed by coming to my *loka* and the rest will be removed by touching the dust of my residence and permitted his entry. At last *Indra* came there and was very much pleased seeing the goddess *Kālī.*[326]

Kālisthāna Vanranam

The *Mahādeva* has described *Kālīs* residence[327] to *Nārada.* The city is on all sides surrounded by the ocean of sweet water and is protected by the *Bhairavas.* The city is consisted of so many valuable jewels and gems. There is a wall around the city having four gates in the four directions. In the middle of the city there is a palace made of jewels and of gold. There is a throne placed on he shoulders of so many lions and goddess is sitting on.[328] She has got 64 maid servants called *Yoginīs,* who performed all the duties pertaining to this city. Devī is enjoying with *Sadāśiva.* The palace is well-protected by the *Bhairavas.* and so many *Brahmās, Viṣṇus* and other gods are waiting for her looks.

In the north there is a *Pārijāta Vana,*[329] beautiful with blosomed flowers, and singing sounds of birds. In the east there is a tank, beautiful with golden lotuses, birds and bees as well as with the flowers of *Champaka,* and *Ashoka.* Its banks and steps and made of costly jewels. In the south *Sadā Śiva* lives in various forms and manifestations and Devi enjoys with him.[330]

Kāmarūpa Māhātmyam

After the death of *Satī,* his wife, Śiva was suffering fom the pangs of separation. At that time all the gods headed by *Viṣṇu* and *Brahmā* appeared there at *Kāmarūpa* where *Śiva* was staying those days Having come to know about his pitiable condition due to the separation from his wife *Satī* and *Śiva*' earnest desire to see or to procure her (*Satī or Prākṛtī)* again as his wife, *Brahmā* and *Viṣṇu* both advised him to perform penances at *Kamārūpa.*[331] *Śiva* acted according to their advice and was successful to have a look of the goddess. He asked Her to be born again as his wife, and she also promised to be born in the *Himālayas,*[332] as daughter of *Himālaya* and *Menakā,* and to be married to *Śiva.* After some time *Gangā* was born first and was devoted to *Śiva,* and later on *Durgā* was born and married to Siva.[333]

Ultimately *Śiva* was successful to have *Satī* again as his wifc, by performing penance in the Kāmarūpa.[334] Similarly if anyone else performs *Tapa* at *Kāmarūpa,* will always be sauccessful in his mission. It is a Mahapīth, and Mukti is given to everybody who leaves his body here.[335] At *Kāmarūpa* there is Yoni-symbol representing the goddess[336] and is considered the best place for pilgrimage in the world as the ten *Mahāvidyās* also stay here. One should go there and worship the goddess with devotion to attain both worldly enjoyments and final salvation.

Bhagavatī Gitā

It is a part of Mahābhāgavat Purāṇa[337] and deals with the philosophy of *Śakti* cult. Devi herself taught it to *Himālaya,* her father. She revealed herself before her father by disclosing that she is none except Brahman, *i.e.*, Final authority and enjoying everbliss. *Śakti* is associated with *Śiva* and is all knowing.[338] Seeing her *Virātswaroopa,* a fearful form, Himavān was frightened and requested for a charming appearance of the goddess[339] and then saw her beautiful form. She preaches the cult of *Bhakti,* the only and the best solution for the attainment of salvation.[340] Here it can be compared with *Bhagavadgītā*, where Ātman is said to be of the nature of Cit (conciousness) and pure and free from birth and death. Ātman is one only,[341] and resides in all the bodies. Devi Gītā praises the *Jñāna*, and also describes in detail the science of embryology.[342] Devi says here that all this world and the so-called enjoyments are not true like a dream. One should be wholeheartedly devoted to the goddess, to be freed from worldly bondage.[343] She as *Śakti* is pervaded in everyone and from time to time she helps them in wining the war between good and bad.[344] Here we can see that the author has borrowed the ideas and the words, even the verses from the Bhagavadgītā.[345]

The *Mahābhāgavata Prāṇa* also identifies *Durgā* or *Parā Śaktī* with *Brahman*[346] She is present in whole of the world in the form of all gods. She is having the *Sacchidānnda* form[347] and is known only by the *Vedas*. She is the progenitor of the worlds and the beings and She makes the world be illuminated by her own lustre.[348] She is *cit Śakti Spanda Śakti* and *Māyā* [349] She is the only authority to give salvation to all the beings and is the presiding deity of the Mantras.[350] Though called *Mūla Prakṛti* she is identified with Brahman and is the instigation of all the agencies of creation, preservation and destruction of the world. She may be called in this form as Jagdambā, the world Mother.[351] The author throughout the text calls her as *Pūrṇa Prakṛti*, who divided herself in five modifications, viz. Gangā, Savitrī, Durgā, Lakshmī, and Saraswatī.[352] Even Śiva himself surrenders before her by saying that she is an independent sovereign power,[353] with nobody to check her. She in the form of Mohini, attracts everyone, including *Śiva* and *Viṣṇu*. Her name is *Mahākalī* [354] and Her abode is called *Paramapada*, given to her devotees only.[355]

In the *Mahābhāgavata Purāṇa*, *Śakti* first of all, as Sati, is the wife of *Śiva*,[356] To destroy the sacrifice of *Dakṣa*, she became Kali[357] and burnt herself in the sacrificial fire, and in the next birth she was called Uma, Girijā, *Pārvatī*,[358] as the daughter of Himvān and Menakā. She is the wife of *Śiva* and his permanant associate in the form of *Ardha-nārīswara*.[359] At the time of creation she is *Prākṛtī*, while in the *Pralaya* period and as a controllor of the world, she is *Brahman*.[360] As an independent goddess, she is called *Durgā*. the manifestation of her *Brahman* aspect.[361] When she killed the demons, *Caṇḍa, Muṇḍa, Śumbha, Niśumbha,* and *Raktabīja* etc., she is called *Kātyāyanī* [362] and *Ambikā* In *Dvāpara* age to destroy the demons and to help the Pāṇḍavas, Devī incarnated herself as *Kṛṣṇa*.[363] As the fulfiller of the desires of her devotees she is called *Kāmeśwari*, the presiding deity of *Kāmarūpa*, also known as *Kāmākhya*.[364] The *Purāṇa* deals mainly the three manifestations of *Devī*, first as daughter of *Daksha*, *Satī*', second as wife of *Śiva—Girijā, Umā*, and *Pārvatī*', and third as *Kṛṣṇa* and last of all identifies all these, with *Para Śakti* or *Para Brahman*, whose grace is enjoyed by the beings all over the universe.

Foot Notes

1. Hazra (R.C.), Studies in the Upa-purāṇas, Vol. I. p. 26.
2. Bṛhaddharma P.—after mentioning that the Upa-purāṇas are 18.1.25-27
3. Hazra (R.C.), Studies in the Upa-Purāṇas, Vol. I,p.1-21.
4. Ibid.
   (i) Kūrma P. I.1.17-20. quoted in Niytāchara-Pradipa by Raghunandan; in Vira-Mitrodaya by Hemādri, and in Śabda Kalpadrūma.
   (ii) Saura Saṁhitā of Skanda P.
   (iii) Skanda P. V. iii. Revākhaṇḍa I. 46-52.
   (iv) Reva Māhātmya.
   (v) Skanda P., Prabhāsa Khaṇḍa I.2.11-15.
   (vi) Śiva Māhātmya. Khaṇḍa of Sūta Saṁhitā of Skanda P. I.13b.18.
   (vii) Garuḍa P. I.223.17-20.
   (viii) Padma P.—Pātāla Khaṇḍa, 3.94b-98.
   (ix) Devī Bhāgavata, 1.3.13-16.
   (x) Bṛhaddharma P. I.25.23-26.
   (xi) Brahma Vai. p. quoted in Vīrā Mitrodaya and in Bhaktiratnākāra.
   (xii) Ekāmra P. I. 20b-23.
5. Mention of 18 Upa-purāṇas. Kūrma P. quoted by the Nibandhakāras before 850 A.D.
   (i) Raghunandana—in his Smṛti Tattva (1.7.92-98).
   (ii) Mitra Mishra—in his Vira Mitrodaya (Paribhāsā Prakāsh),
   (iii) Hemādri in Caturvarga—Cintāmaṇi, I.p. 532-33. II.i,p.21,
   (iv) Narsiṁha Vājapeyin Nityāchāra Pradīp, I, p. 19.
   (v) Vallālasena in Dānasāgara, p. 3.
6. Hazra (R.C). Studies in the Upa-purāṇas, Vol. I,p.25.
7. *Ibid.*
8. Śaura P. 9.4-5.
9. Hazra (R.C.), Studies in the Upa-purāṇas, Vol. I,p.26.
10. Mārkandeya P. Chs. 81-93.
    Vāmana P. Chs. 17-21 and Chs. 51-56.

Varāha P. Chs. 21-28 and Chs. 90-96.
Kūrma P. I. chs. 11-12.
Skanda P. varios sections.
Śiva P. Umā Saṁhitā—Vāyu Saṁhitā.
Brahma Vaivrta P. prakṛti Khaṇḍa.
Devī Bhāgavata P. as a whole it is a compendium cf Śakti-worship.

11. Hazra (R.C.). Studies in īhe Upa- purāṇas.Vol.II.p.2.
12. *Ibid* p. 14.
13. *Ibid*. p. 36.
14. Devī P. ch. 79
15. *Ibid*. ch. 10.
16. *Ibid*., ch. 30.
17. *Ibid*. ch. 22.
18. *Ibid*. ch. 72.
19. Devī. P. ch. 108-110.
20. *Ibid* ch. 38,
21. *Ibid*. I.1.
22. Hazra (V.C.). Studies in the Upa-purāṇas. Vol. II, p. 37.
23. *Ibid*. Vol. 11.p.67.
24. *Ibid*.
25. It is only in the Ekāmra P.(A work of Orissa) that the devī Purāṇa has been included in the list of 18 Upa-purāṇas.—*Ibid*. Vol II, 1.p. 13.
26. Hazra (R.C.). Studies in the Upa-purāṇas. Vol. II. p. 77.
27. Farquhar, Outline of the religious literature of India, p.148, and 179-180.
28. Studies in the upa-puraṇas, Vol. II, p. 77.
29. *Ibid*, p.90.
30. Daśa-Kumāra-Charitam, Ucchvasa VI. p. 149.
31. Hazra (R.C.), Studies in the Upa-purāṇas, Vol. II. p. 143
32. *Ibid*.
33. Kṛtya Ratnākara, p. 358:
34. *Indian Historical Quarterly*, Vol. XXIII. No. 4. p. 322.
35. Devī P. 39.14; 42.9.
36. (a) Barua (B.K.), A Cultural History of Assam. Vol. 1, p.141.
(b) Barua (K.L.), Early History of Kāmarupa, p. 163.
(c) Hazra (R.C.), Studies in the Upa-purāṇas, Vol. II, p. 245.
(d) Gode (P.K.), Studies in Indian Literary Studies, Vol.V., p.203.

Under Singhi Jain Series No. 37. (There is a long discussion by the learned scholar about the date of Kālīkā Purāṇa. He has also concluded that the Purāṇa was composed before 1000 A.D.).

37. Kālīkā P, chapters—1-50
38. Kālīkā P chapters—fifty onwards describe the goddesses viz. Kālī, Mahāmāya, Durgā, Kāmākhyā, Ugrachaṇḍā, Matangi and so on.
39. Hazra (R.C.), Studies in the Upa-purāṇa, Vol. II, p. 235.
40. Kakati (B.K.), The Mother goddess Kāmākhya. Preface p. vi.
41. Dunken (J), article in 'Purāṇa', Jan. 1963. p. 25.
42. Kālikā Purāṇa, ch. 71.
43. Hazra (R.C.), Studies in the Upa-Purāṇas, Vol. II, 261.
44. Bṛahaddharma P. I.25.20.
45. Hazra (R.C.), Studies in the Upa-purāṇas, Vol. II, 261.
46. Mahābhāgavata P. 15.16.
47. *Ibid.* 81.13.14;81.32-35.
48. Hazra (R.C.), Stūdies in the Upa-purāṇas, Vol. II.p.83, P-277-83.
49. Mahābhāgavata. 67.61.
50. *Ibid.* 8.72; 12.37; Chs. 44-45.
51. *Ibid.* Ch. 43 mentions Devī's Purāṇic and Tantric forms.
52. *Ibid.* 8.77-82.
53. *Ibid.* 7.63-64; 10.42 and 64 and so on.

Hazra (R.C.), Studies in the Upa-purāṇas,Vol. II, p. 283.

54. *Ibid.* Vol. II, p. 90.
55. Devī P. 5.60.
56. *Ibid.*
57. *Ibid.* 6.11.
58. *Ibid.* 6.19-34.
59. Devī P. 9.54.
60. *Ibid.* 2.21.
61. *Ibid.* 2.21a.
62. *Ibid*; 2.33.
63. *Ibid.* 6.32.
64. *Ibid.* ch. 9.
65. Devī P. 77.7-11.
66. *Ibid.* 76.21,
67. Sapta Śati 2.13.
68. Devī P. 127.47-60.
69. *Ibid.* 127.45-48.
70. Sapta Śati—2.9-19.
71. Devī Bhāgavata P. 7.31, 25-54.
72. Devī Bhāgavatas P. 12.8.51-57.
73. Devī P. 17.19-31.
74. *Ibid.* 17.19-26.
75. *Ibid.* 17.19.
76. *Ibid.* 36.4.

77. Ibid. 36.5-6.
78. *Ibid.* 36.9.
79. *Ibid.* 36.11.
80. *Ibid.* 36.13-14.
81. *Ibid.* 36.17.
82. *Ibid.* 36.19-25.
83. *Ibid.* 36.32-34. 18.
84. *Ibid.* 73-79.
85. Devī P. 37.80-81.
86. *Ibid.* 37.82.87.
87. *Ibid.* 37.88-91.
88. *Ibid.* 98.3-6.
89. *Ibid.* 98.7-15.
90. *Ibid.* 6.41-43.
91. Ibid. 127.174-75.
92. Devī Bhāgāvata P. VIII. i. 24-30.
93. Devī P, 95.29-30.
94. *Ibid.* 95.38.
95. *Ibid.* 95.39-40.
96. *Ibid.* 95.41-42.
97. *Ibid.* 95.43.
98. *Ibid.* 15.2,
99. *Ibid.* 15.8,
100. *Ibid.* 15.8; 9.
101. *Ibid.* 15.10.
102. *Ibid.* 16.16.
103. Devī P. 89.3;27.1-2.
104. *Ibid.* 89.20.
105. *Ibid.* 80.12-13.
106. *Ibid.* 89.2.
107. *Ibid.* 89.3-6,16.
108. *Ibid.* 89.8.
109. *Ibid.* 89.4, 14.
110. *Ibid.* 89.12-13, 3, 18-19.
111. *Ibid.* 89.13.
112. *Ibid.*
113. *Ibid.* 81.7.
114. *Ibid.* 89.9.
115. *Ibid.*
116. *Ibid.*
117. *Ibid.* 89.7, 17, 22-23.
118. *Ibid.* 76.21.
119. Devī P. 92.9-11.
120. *Ibid.* 7.20
121. *Ibid.* 7.21-44; 7.1.7.
122. *Ibid.* 12.1-35.
123. *Ibid.* 12.63-64.
124. *Ibid.* 12.70.
125. *Ibid.* 13.1-28.
126. Devī P. 83.46.
127. *Ibid.* 83.66.
128. *Ibid.* 83. 47-113,
129. *Ibid.* 39. -121-22.
130. *Ibid.* 39. 136-39.
131. *Ibid.* 39.166.
132. Devī P. 39.171; 176-77; 179.
133. *Ibid.* 93. 5-6.
134. *Ibid.* 93.22.28-39.
135. *Ibid.* 93.16.
136. *Ibid.* 93.58.
137. *Ibid.* 93.61-102.
138. *Ibid.* 84.21.
139. *Ibid.* 84.22-26.
140. Devī P. 73.58.
141. *Ibid.* 72.124; 83.63.
142. *Ibid.* 72.144-150.
143. *Ibid.* 72.127.
144. *Ibid.* 6.23; 6-26-31, Sapta Sati 10.5.
145. *Ibid.* 81.4-6.
146. *Ibid.* 81.11-12.
147. *Ibid.* 16.14-15; 117.9-10.
148. *Ibid.* 67.39.

149. Mukerji (R.K.), The Cultūre and art of India, p. 168.
150. Devī P. 22.5-6; 23-24; 24.17; 51.4-5; 88.4; 89.19; 91.1.
151. *Ibid.* 22.19; 35.17-18; 90.21; 91.61; 93.165;
152. *Ibid.* 1.55; 7.22; 8.6; 10.9; 12.26; 35.23; 72.26; 73.8; 82.11; 93.45.
153. Hazra (R.C.), Studies in the Upa-purānas, Vol. II, p. 92.
154. *Ibid.* Vol. II, p. 92-93.
155. Devī. P. 6.31; 39.25;9.65; 32.43; 39.146; 55.856.22; 88.1;91.14.
156. *Ibid.* 7.65-66; 9.56; 68; 26.21-22; 29.14; 77.21-22; 98.40; 93.267 and so on.
157. Devī P. 50 iii-18.28, 30: 118.6; Mahāmānsa in Homa 9.68-69.
158. Hazra (R.C.), Studies in the Upa-purāṇas. Vol II. p.195.
159. Kālikā P. I. I-20. 160. *Ibid.* chs. 1-45.
161. *Ibid.* ch. 5.8. 162. *Ibid.* chs.9.24.
163. *Ibid.* ch. 5.5; 9.1-26.
164.Mahạbhāgavata P. & Kālikā P. 41.1-50.
165. Hazra (R.C.), Studies in the Upa-purāṇas, Vol II, p. 198. Kālikā P. 5.3.
166. Kālikā Purāṇa 8.9-10.
167. Mārkaṇḍeya P. 81. 41-42.
168. *Ibid.* 81-44.
169. Devī Bhāgavata, III. 2.25-40.
170. *Ibid.* III. 3. 54-56. Kālikā P. 12.5-38.
171. Kālikā P. 5.8, 6.74, 24.9-27.
172. *Ibid.* 5.15-50. 173. Kālikā P. 5.52.60.
174. *Ibid.* 6.61-74. 175. *Ibid.* 8.12-26; 50-57.
176. *Ibid.* 24.11-23; 47.83-85.
177. *Ibid.* 5.8.; 48.34. 178. *Ibid.* 5.65-71.
179. *Ibid.*6.7-10. 180. *Ibid.* 6.61-74.
181. *Ibid.* 8.12, 50-53. 182. *Ibid.* 12.5-38,
183. *Ibid.* 52.36. 184. *Ibid.* 62.5.
185. Kālikā P. II. 17-20. 186. *Ibid.* 16.49.50.
187. *Ibid.* 18.37-54. 188. *Ibid.* 42.1-42.
189. *Ibid.* 42.47-48.
190. *Ibid.* 43.50-53; 44.10-11; 45.13-15.

191. *Ibid.* 46.44-61.
192. *Ibid.* 47.21-22; 47.50-57.
193. *Ibid.* 8.50; 55.1-30; 60.52.
194. Kālikā P. 12.65; 50.30-34; 61.6-13.
195. *Ibid.* 55.25-35; 62.16. 196. *Ibid.* 56.16.
197. *Ibid.* 56.35-45. 198. *Ibid.* 57.1-2; 1-22,
199. *Ibid.* 60.41-44; 52-59.
200. *Ibid.* 62.9. 201. *Ibid.* 62.16.
202. *Ibid.* 62.18-22. 203. *Ibid.* 62.54-63; 88.
204. Kālikā P. 62.70-79. 205. *Ibid.* 63.93-95.
206. This is to some extent resembles to the description given in the Viṣṇu-dharmatra Purāṇa.
207. Kālikā P. 63.71-74. 208. *Ibid.* 63.78-86.
209. Sapta Śati. 5.87-91. 210. Kālikā P. 83.13-65
211. *Ibid.* 212. *Ibid.* 81.20.
213. *Ibid.* 81.21.
214. *Ibid.* Tārā Tantra Śākta Pramoda, P. 131
215. Kālikā P. 83.52
216. *Ibid.* 40.52; 83.53-54; 66,
217. *Ibid.* 80.61-64. 218. *Ibid.* 63.43-45.
219. *Ibid.* 63.45-46. 220. *Ibid.* 75,74.
221. Kālikā P. chs. 66-67. 222. *Ibid.*
223. *Ibid.* Tripurā Rahasya, p. 2.26-32.
224. Kālikā P. 74.124 225. *Ibid.* 75.66.
226. *Ibid.* 60.40-59.
227. *Ibid.* 64.1-6; 49-63; 76.36-40; 82.75-63.
228. *Ibid.* 64.78-79. 229. *Ibid.* 65.3.
230. *Ibid.* 65.9-15. 231. *Ibid.* 66.22
232. Kālikā P. 76 87-90; chapter 76 is simply the glorification of the goddess Kāmākhyā.
233. *Ibid.*chs.—66-67.Tripurā Rahasya (Mahātmya Khaṇḍa), The Kāshi Sanskrit Series, ed. by Pandit Mukunda Lal Shastri
234. Yogini Tantra. 1.6.1.7.
235. Bhandarkar, Vaishnavism, Śaivism and other religions, p. 146.
236. Tripurā Rahasya. 57-66.
237. Ibid. 59.3. 238. Ibid.
239. Kālikā Purāṇa 1941.
240. Briffault: Mothers, Vol. III, p. 169-70.
241. Kālikā Purāṇa 78-86.

242. *Ibid.* 67-55.
243. *Ibid.* 68-89; 62.66.
244. *Ibid* 78.100.
245. *Ibid.* 78.93
246. *Ibid.* 78.125.
247. *Ibid.* 78.87.
248. *Ibid.* 56-7.
249. Kālikā P. 56-7.
250. *Ibid.* 57.56.
251. *Ibid.* 80.15.
252. *Ibid.* 18.42-43.
253. *Ibid*
254. *Ibid.* chs. 37-41.
255. Mankad (D.R.), Purāṇic Chronology p. 225.
256. Mankad (D.R.), Purāṇic Chronology, p. 226;Kālikā P.37.35-52.
257. *Ibid.* p. 228.
258. *Ibid*, p. 229. Kālikā P. 39.16.60, 167; 40.1. (for Naraka) 41.11;49 (for Anarakasura).
259. *Ibid.* p. 229. Kālikā P. 39.101-125.152-53.
260. *Ibid.* p. 230. Kālikā P. 39.153; 167.
261. *Ibid.* p. 227; 231. Kālikā P. 40,2-18; 78;41.32-35.
262. Mankad (D.R.), Purāṇic Chronology, p. 227; 231. Kālikā P. 51-80-110
263. Kālikā P. 37.35-52.
264. *Ibid.* 39.153; 167.
265. *Ibid.* 60.2-18; 7S; 41.32-35.
266. Kakati (B.K.) The Mother goddess Kāmākhyā, p. 18.
267. Yogini Tantra. kakati (B.K.) The Mother goddess Kāmākhyā, p. 18.
268. Kālikā P. ch. 85.
269. Kakati (B.K.), The Mother goddess Kāmākhyā, p. 18-19.
270. Kakati (B.K.) The Mother goddess Kāmākhyā, p. 16.
271. J. Muir, Original Sanskrit Text, Vol. IV. 1864, p. 370, 160. 311-312.
272. Kakati (B.K.) The Mother, goddess Kāmākhya, p. 17.
273. Barua (B.K.). A Cultural history of Āssam. Vol. 1, p. 147-149. Barua (K.L.) Early History of Kāmarūpa p. 14.
274. Kakati (B.K.) The Mother Goddess Kāmākhyā, p. 35-36.
275. Mahā-bhāgavata, I. 1-4.
276. *Ibid.*
277. *Ibid*

278. *Ibid.* 15.16
279. *Ibid.* 18.14
280. Mahābhāgāvata 15.17.
281. *Ibid.* 18.14, also Brahma Vaivarta P. II.1.1-20.
282. *Ibid.* 15.9.
283. *Ibid.* 15.16.
284. *Ibid.*
285. *Ibid.* 15.17-20.
286. *Ibid.* 15.50-51.
287. *Ibid.* 15.37-39.
288. *Ibid.* 18.3-8.
289. Gītā 10.1-32.
290. Māhābhāgavata 18.14.
291. *Ibid.* 18.36.
292. *Ibid.* 18.1-43.
293. Mahābhārata P. 56.72-73.
294. *Ibid.* 56-75.
295. *Ibid.* 56.71.
296. *Ibid.* chs. 37-48 only
297. *Ibid.* chs 50-54 only
298. *Ibid.* chs 55-58 only
299. *Ibid.* chs. 60-63 only.
300. *Ibid.* 88.120-121.
301. Mahābhāgavata P. 49.58-59.
302. *Ibid.* 49.50; 55.58; 52-28.
303. *Ibid.* 56.36; 40-45-70-7S.
304. *Ibid.* 57.12-24
305. *Ibid.* 57.24
306. *Ibid.* 49.15-30.
307. *Ibid.* 49.18-30.
308. *Ibid.* 49.41.
309. *Ibid.* 49.29-50.
310. *Ibid.* 50.1; 61.
311. *Ibid.* 49-58.
312. Mahābhāgavata P. 51.18; 32; 53.14; 55.1.40; 49.28.
313. *Ibid.* 51.16; 24.
314. *Ibid.* chs. 49-54; 52.10-12.
315. *Ibid.* 58.1-53; 57.23.
316. *Ibid.* 51.18; 32; 53.14; 55.1; 58.49-52.
317. *Ibid.* 38.1-55.
318. *Ibid.* 38.1-55.
319. *Ibid.* chs. 39-40-41.
320. *Ibid.* ch. 44.1-31.
321. Mahābhāgavata P. 41.1-24.
322. *Ibid.* 60.1.-32
323. *Ibid.* 61.1-65.
324. *Ibid.* 62.1-27.
325. *Ibid.* 63.1-20
326. Mahābhāgavata P. 59.63.28-33.
327. *Ibid.* 1-32.
328. *Ibid.*59-11-13.
329. *Ibid.* 59.26-30.
330. *Ibid.* 59, 32.
331. Mahābhāgavata Chs. 12; 76-78.
332. *Ibid.* 12.11; 29 31.
333. *Ibid.* 12, 42-43.
334. *Ibid.* 12.29-31; 76.35-36.
335. *Ibid.* 12.35-49; 56.2.
336. *Ibid.* 76.19-20; 71.22-29.
337. *Ibid.* chs. 17-19
338. *Ibid.* 15.16-19.
339. *Ibid.* 15.22-35.
340. *Ibid.* 15.60-72.

341. Mahābhāgavata P. 16.3-6,14.
342. *Ibid,* 17. 1-31
343. *Ibid.* 17.32-51; 18.12; 34.
344. *Ibid.* 18, 17-20.
345. For example see the verses 18.38-40; 43 with Gīta verses 9.29, 30, 27. and 18.65.
346. *Ibid.* 1.29; 35; 46; 2.17; 5.18; 11.3; 21-26.
347. *Ibid.* 1.31. 40-41; 3.13-14.
348. *Ibid.* 1.25-27.
349. *Ibid.* 1.34; 5.27; 43 39-40.
350. *Ibid.* 2.17-19.
351. *Ibid.* 3.1-4; 26-31.
352. *Ibid.* 3.26; 5.1.
353. Mahābhāgavata P. 8.89-90.
354. *Ibid.* 20.34-36.
355. *Ibid.*48.21-22.
356. *Ibid.* 3.7-8; 4.24-27.
357. *Ibid.*8.46-53; 101-106; 8.22-13; 33-37; 77-80; 56.23.
358. *Ibid.*22.57-58.
359. *Ibid.*29.14; 81;10.
360. *Ibid.*43.30-39.
361. *Ibid.*1-40-55; 2.5-5; 43-41-45.
362. *Ibid.*44.9-16; 52.10.
363. *Ibid.* 55.1.
364. *Ibid.* 56.17-26; 76.15-19.

two

The Tāntric Śakti-Cult

The Tantras

The word *Tantra* is derived from the root *Tan* meaning to draw out, or to spread.[1] The significance is clearly brought out by the worlds like *Tantu*; what is spun out like a thread, a strand, and (*Tana*) the body, in which the spirit has spread out or revealed itself. *Tantra* stands for ritual in general, the art of religiōn, to which every religion of the world, ancient and modern is associated with one form or other. We can say that ritualism has been the body (*Tanu*) in which the spirit of religion has most commonly manifested. As there is no smoke without fire, it would be in order to say that there is no ritual without religion, and wherever there is ritual, there is *Tantra*.

The Balanced Indian opinion through the ages has always given a high place to *Tantra*. The word *Āgama*, which stands indifferently for the *Veda* and the *Tantra*,[2] has been adopted by common consent for indicating authoritative tradition *Kullūka Bhāṭṭa*, the celebrated commentator on *Manusmṛti* does not step outside the pale of orthodoxy when he asserts that Ś*ruti* is two-fold, *Vaidika* and *Tntrika*.[3] Lord *Śrīkṛṣṅa* in the Bhāgavata Purāṇa speaks that religious practice or *Ācāra* is of three kinds, *Vaidika*,

Tāntrika and Miṣra (*composite*).[4] The generality of Hindu observance to-day could only be classified as *Miśra*, so inextricably are the *Vaidika* and *Tāntrika* elements mixed up in it. The *Veda* and *Tantra* do indeed constitute the warp and woof of Hindu thought and usage.

Antiquity of the Tantras

The *tantras* have been in prominence at a later date than that of the *Vedas* is accepted by all.[5] Though the *Tantras* claim their origin from the Vedas,[6] But the Tantric form of *Sādhanā* probably came into special prominence when on the one hand, the elaborate details enjoined by the *Vedic* sacrifices, taking a long-time to be performed, could not be accomplished by the people of feeble attainments, and when on the other, the *Upaniṣadic* method of acquisition of transcendent knowledge surpassed the intellects and equipments of the common people.[7] The *Purāṇas* were at this time preaching the *Bhakti* cult in order to place before the masses an easy method capable of being grasped and followed by all. Then the *tantras* offered themselves to the people, containing within them the essentials of *Vedic* sacrifices and oblations, the essence of the monotheistic philosophy of the *Upaniṣads* the *Bhakti* cult preached by the *Purāṇas*, the *Yoga* method propounded by *Patañjali*, and the *Mantra* element of the *Atharva Veda*.[8]

According to Carl Clemen[9]· Tantra means literary production dealing with religion, philosophy and natural sciences and is of a later date than the *Vedic* literature," In its narrower acceptation it means the writings, which treat in a certain way, of religion, ritual, conduct of life, medicine, magic etc.[10] The history of the *Tantras* goes back to the 7th century and come down up to 19th According to Farquhar the period ranging from 500 A.D. to 900 A.D.[11] is called a *Śakta* period. It is a period when *Śaktism* was prevalent in India and the works like the Purāṇas, Upapurāṇs, sectarian *Upaniṣads* as well as the old and important *Tantras,* were written.[12] Orthodox people attribute a divine-origin to the *Tantras* and thus claim for these a oary antiquity. While some of these Tantric works may be fairly old, but all the tantric works cannot be supposed to be so. We may agree with Cintaharan Cakravarti about the date of the *Tantras,*[13] when he says, that as a matter of fact no particular age is possible to be assigned to the *Tantra* literature, which took a long range of time to develop. In reality the age of each individual work has to be determined on the basis of the available evidences, both internal and external'.

Thought the worship of the goddess, is amplified in the *Itih*āsas like the *Mah*ābhārāta *and in the Purāṇas,* still the most extensive exposition is found only in the *Tantras*. It is called *Tantra* because it gives us extensive knowledge relating to the *Tattvas* and the *Mantras,* and leads us to salvation.[14] The special feature of the *Tantras* is that these are open to the persons of all castes and sexes and are not subject to restrictions of the *Vaidika* religion.

Let us not accept for a moment the facile theory that the *Vedas* and the *Tantras* conflict with one another. They do conflict, if at all, in the same manner in which *Śruti* and *Smṛti* conflict, and in which the *Vedas* and the *Purāṇas* conflict. The *Veda* is definitely supreme and eternal and if anything conflicts with it, either it must be explained or given up. The *Veda* is the world as idea in the cosmic mind of the creation, and the *Tantra* is an amplification of the *Veda*.

Śakti

The supreme deity of the *Tantras* is known as *Śakti,* inseperable from *Śiva*. *Śakti* and *Śiva* are not two or double starts, but are ultimately one and the same. These are the two[15] modes of the manifestation of the eternal and infinite *Brahman, as Puruṣa and Prakrti* (but not that of

Sāṅkhya) *i.e.* Mother and spirit, whom the Tantras describe as Śiva and *Śakti.*[16]

Tantras hold that *Śiva* and *Śakti* are inseparable like heat from fire, whiteness from milk, sweatness from sugar, luminosity from light, and weight form natural bodies.[17] It is the *Śakti* in the *Tantras* which is said to have brought the universe into existence,[18] She governs the universe and overwhelms us with wonder and awe. In other words it can be said that *Śakti* denotes *Brahman* and His divine energy, glorifying the mother aspect of the God.

1. *Śakti* is the reverse of the concept of Śiva *who is* Sthāṇu, and immovable. In one respect, it is the concept of Divine Energy in its static aspect, motionless, inhert, and without agitation; whereas, *Śakti* is the concept of Divine Energy in its dynamic aspect.[19] *Śakti* is the personification of the Divine Energy that has brought the universe into existence; and that preserves it from disruptive forces. In other words, *Śakti* is the creative and preservative energy of Brahmans.[20]

2. *Śiva* is the emblem of the destructive forces that lie dorment in the univeres.[21] Goddess *Śakti* is the fullest conception of *Brahman* in all its aspects, i.e. as Creator, Preserver, and Destroyer of the unvierse.[22] Creation is a mode of Divine existence, and Divine energy sustains the universe that binds the atoms with atoms. Again destruction is also an aspect of Divine energy that goes hand in hand with the creative energy. Thus the creative, preservative and destructive forces are but the three aspects of Divine Energy that exists in *Brahman. Mahā Śakti* is the complete perception of *Brahman* with the three *Guṇas—Sattva, Rajas* and *Tamas,* and it is the personification of the creative, preservative, and destructive forces of the universe.[23]

Śakti is also the power of every God like *Indra, Viṣṇu* etc., in other words, she manifests herself as *Śakti,* power, force, or energy in everything and in every being. This universe is the manifestation of *Śākti.*[24] Now this is the concept of the *Śakti* conceived in the *Tantras*. A *Śākta* worships *Brahman* as *Śakti* or as He appears through the manifestation of His Divine energy, conceived in the *Tantras as Mahāśakti.*[25] God alongwith his Divine energy or attributes (which alone reveal us His existence), conceived as *Mahāśakti* or the fountain head of all energy, is perhaps the most profound philosophical concept of *Brahman*, preached in the *Tantrā.*

KĀLI, THE GODDESS OF THE TANTRĀS

The *svarūpa* of this *Mahāśakti* has been revealed in *tantric* texts, in the *Dhyāna mantras* of *Kālikā.* The *Mahānirvāna Tantra* says that She is the great progenitor of the minutest and biggest things in the universe, and both the animate and the inanimate beings. This universe is begotten of Her free will, who is the beginning of all. The *Vidyās* and the Trinity, all owe their existence to Her. She is cognisant of the entire universe but none in the universe knows Her.[26] She is *Kālī, Tarā, Shoḍaśī, Bhuvaneśwari, Dhumāvatī, Bagalā, Bhairavī, Chinnamasta, Mātaṅgī and Kamalā.* She is surrounded on all sides by the gods and goddesses. She is at the same time the grossest and subtlest matter. She is devoid of all dimensions and yet takes various forms. For the fulfilment of the desires of the *Sādhakas.*[27] She assumes various forms. She appears at times to destroy the *asuras*[28] and assumes four hands and occasionally two, six, eight, ten or thousand hands. She wears various weapons for the maintenance of Her world. She is the great Mother, she being propitiated, all the gods and goddesses are propitiated. She is *Ānanda* itself, or a state of eternal bliss which cannot be conceived by mind or words. When *Pāra Brahman* or *Mahā Kāla* is desirous of creating the universe, the objective world emerges from Him through the *centres* of realisation or cakras. He is ever-existence, pervades all and resides in all. *Mahāśakti* is a *Mahāyogini* connecting the links of creation, preservation and destruction and at the will of the *Mahākāla,* She creates the universe, preserves it and destroys it with all its animate and inanimate objects.[29] The destructive force also is one of Her aspects, as She destroys *Mahākāla* at the time of pralaya, and she is called *Kāli.*[30] She is worshipped as *Ādyā*, being the beginning of all. After *Mahāpralaya* She alone remains the *Tamas or Avyakta Prakṛti* in a state, inconceivable by words or mind. Though formless, she assumes various forms; though without beginning, she is the origin of all,[31] and She is said to be Great Creator, and the Commander of all.

The *Tantras* are unanimous in describing Her, as in a state of eternal bliss and playing in the bosom of *Śiva.*[32] Her feet do not rest on anything except the breast of *Śiva.* She resides in the cremation ground, where all the worldly objects are being reduced to ashes i.e. their seed stage. By Her independent will she begets the universe with all its diversifications, and again sucks them to Her breast in the twinkling of an eye. Unobstructed is Her motion and multifarioas is Her disport. She is black in colour which means that all contradictions like black and white, cold and heat, possible and impossible, birth and death, merge at Her feet,[33] and all distinctions disappear. She is sitting on a corpse which means that she exists in all inanimate objects. She has got terrible teeth yet She is conferring boons to all. She is open mouthed and yet is not affectionate of Her children,[34] bearing as in Her bosom all their belongings, physical, mental, and spiritual. She has a laughting attitude, yet engrossed in wielding the terrible Spirit of Time. She possesses three eyes with which She can peep through the immeasurable Present, Past and Future.[35] She carries in one of Her hands a skull, the receptacle of the Unseen and the seed of the universe. She bears in another hand a cutting instrument which breaks the seeds and puts them in full bloom in the form of the universe. Her hair is dishevelled, *i.e.* She is beyond all bondage and Her outspreading tongue lusciously sucks the blood coming out of the either corner of her fearful mouth. She wears a necklace of letters which are not other than the *Mātṛka Śaktis,* which constitute the unvierse and give it a shape. She is also described as being in a destructive mood standing on the bosom of the *Śiva* with a garland of several heads around Her girdle, in the cremation ground resounding with the howling of jackals.[36] She is neither the knower nor the non-knower. She is *Ānandamayee* where both positivity and negativity meat. *Kālikā* or *Ānandamayee* as She has been called, resides in the heart of *Mahākāla* (the Eternal Time) at Her independent will and appears as *Mahākāli, Mahālakṣmī and Mahāsaraswatī* [37] to fulfil Her sport of Creation, Preservation and Destruction. She herself manifest as these Goddesses and absorbs them in Her at the time of universal dissolution. She is Herself the Maker of the universe and its constituent.[38] She is therefore, worshipped in both the aspects, viz. as the bestower of all the possessions of life and also as the mighty *Śakti* that gives us *kaivaly*[39] *i.e.* oneness with *Brahman*. This is all about *Kālī,* the goddess of the *Tantras*.

Daśa-Mahāvidyās.

The more usual classification of the goddesses, however, is, as the *Mahā-Vidyās*. These are held to be ten in number, and the number being probably selected to match the ten chief incarnations of *Viṣṇu*. These are called Māhā*vidyās* as sources of all that is to be known.[40] These are the most important deities of the *Tantras*. They have all different attributes, and are thus designated[41]:—

1. *Kālī* (sometiems called *Śyāmā*), is black in colour, and fierce in character.
2. *Tārā*, is a benign manifestation
3. *Soḍaśī*, the goddess as a beautiful girl of 16 (also called *Tripuā*).
4. *Bhuvaneśvarī*

5. *Bhairavī.*
6. *Chinna-mastakā,* a naked goddess holding in one hand a bloodstained scimitar and in the other she owns her headless trunk.
7. *Dhūmāvatī,*
8. *Bagalā or Bagalā-mukhī*
9. *Mātaṅgī.*
10. *Kamalātimkā or Kamalā.*

Of these the first two are especially the *Mahāvidyās,* the next five on the *Vidyās,* and the last the three *Siddhavidyās.* As we have already discussed the chief of the *Mahāvidyās* viz. Kālī, now we give a brief description of the other *Mahāvidyās* in the above-said order.

Tārā

In the *Tantras* she is a goddess, who leads to the other shore.[42] She has a dual aspect, the one fierceful and the other pacified and luminous. She is also worshipped in Buddhism. She is of dark blue complexion whereas *Kālī,* already mentioned is of dark colour.[43] *Tārā* places her left leg on the breast of *Śiva,* who is lying like a corpse. She is of short stature with a protruding and she has a terrible appearance as dressed in tiger skin; and wearing on her neck a garland of severed human heads. She is in the prime of her youth and is adorned with *pañcmudrās.* She is possessed of four hands and her tongue is held out a bit and wears single braid of matted hair on her head.[44] The Ṛsi Akṣhobhya resides in her forehead. Her complexion is as effulgent as that of the newly rising sun. She is three-eyed and stands in the midst of a funeral pyre[45] and the range of her teeth seems to be terrible She is laughing, engrossed in her emotion, and is decked with ornaments worn by the women. She takes her stand on a white lotus in the midst of a wide expanse of water.[46]

Ṣoḍaśī

She is third Mahā*vidyā.*[47] and is as resplendant as the

newly rising sun. She is also three-eyed and holds in her four hands noose, goad, arrow and bow. She is seated on a pedestal comprising of *Brahmā, Viṣṇu, Rudras, Īśwara a* (*Idra*) and *Sadāśiva* and the alter on which she takes her seat is *Śiva* himself. On the alter is *Mahākāla* with whom the *Mahāvidyā* sports in joy. She, the goddess of sixteen, is the power of Śiva and is ruling over the three worlds. She is identified with *Tripurasundarī*[48] also.

Bhuvaneśvarī

She is the fourth *Mahāvidyā,* and is considered the consort of *Śiva*. She takes care of the three worlds and feeds them, that is why she is called Bhuvaneśvarī.[49] Her marvellous radiance illumines the universe. The fruit in her hand shows her as the giver of the fruit of actions. She possesses a crescent on her forehead and a crown over head. Her breasts are full and surcharged with milk. She is three-eyed and her face is ever lit up with smile. In her two hands she holds the noose and the goad and in the other two the pose of granting boons and assurances to her devotees.[50]

Bhairavī or Tripura Bhairavī

The fifth *Mahā*vidy*ā*[51] *Bhairav*ī *is* reddish like the morning sun. She is dressed in a silken cloth and wears a garland of heads on her neck. Her breast is anointed with *Sindūra*. In her four hands she holds a rosary of beads, a book, and the poses of granting boons and assurances. She has a cresent on her forehead, Her three eyes are as beautiful as red lotuses, and there is a bejewelled crown over her head. A mild smile plays on her lips.[52] As a goddess she is *Tripura Bhairav*ī while as a *Mahāvidyā* she is designated as *Bhairavi* only. This is a benign manifestation of Ś*akti* and is considered as the giver of knowledge.[53]

Chinnamastā

The *Sādhaka* should concentrate his mind on a pure

and fully blown lotus in the region of the navel. Within it is the solar region as red as hibiscus and surrounded by three lines, viz., *Sattva, Rajas and Tamas.*[54] Within that region is the goddess *Chinnamastā,* who is an effulgent as tens of millions of the suns together. Her mouth is expansive, terrible to look at, with tongue emitting out. The Goddess is drinking the blood that gushes forth from her throats. Her hair is dishevelled and beautified with many varities of flowers. In her right hand she holds a cutting instrument and wears a garland of human heads. She is naked an feartful in appearance. Her right leg is in front while her left leg is a little behind.[55] The Goddess *Chinnamastā* wears a garland of bones and a serpent in the shape of a sacred thread. She is on a standing posture on *Rati* and K*āma* who are in the attitude of sexual embrance.[56] Her appearance is that of a woman of sixteen years with heavy and rising breasts. On the left and right hand side of the Goddess are two *nāyikas* called *Dākinī* and *Barniṇī.*[57] They also drink the blood streaming out of the Goddess. *Barnini* is red in complexion, naked and with dishevelled hair. In her left hand is the severed head of a man, in her right hand a cutter and she wears a sacrificial thread made of a serpent. She is of a glowing splendour. She is also of sixteen years of age and bedecked with various ornaments, and a garland of bones. The effulgence of *Dākinī* on the left side of the goddess is like that of the sun at the time of the termination of the *kalpa,* resplendent like fire, and her matted hair sparkle like lightning. This *Dākinī* is of three eyes,[58] her rows of teeth are white, face looks terrible, in view of her frightful teeth and her breasts are heavy and prominent. This Dākinī is of very fearful countence, of dishevelled hair and nacked. Her protruding tongue is big. She puts on a garland of human heads on her neck, and holds a human skull in her left hand and a cutter in her right hand. She also quaffs the blood gushing out in another stream from the neck of the Goddess. Both Barniṇī and Dākinī are serving the Goddess.

Dhūmāvati

Dhūmāvatī is pale in complexion,[59] every moving stern and of tall stature. Her cloth is also dirty, her hair disorderly and colourless, she is without teeth and her breasts are hanging. She is in the garb of a window[60] and rides a chariot over which sits a crow. Her two eyes are stern without sight of tenderness. In one of her hands she has a winnowing fan and her other hand is in the attitude of granting boons. Her nose is big, and the body and eye crooked[61] She is afflicted with hunger and thirst, of terrible mien and of quarrel some nature. She is the goddess of poverty, frustration. despair, and is generally identified with misfortune.[62]

Bagalā

The Goddess Bagalā[63] is seated on a throne, placed on an altar beset with gems, in a *maṇḍapa* bespanged with gems and in the midst of an ocean of nectar. She is of yellow countenance and puts on a yellow cloth and is adorned all over with garlands. The Goddess holding the tip of the tongue of the enemy in her left hand, belabours him with a mace taken up in her right hand. She has two hands and is covered all over in yellow.[64]

Mātangī

The Goddess is of dark complexion[65] with a crescent on her forehead, and having three eyes. In her four hands she holds the sowrd, *Kheṭaka,* noose and goad. The Goddess is seated on a throne made of precious stones.

Kamalā

The complexion of the Goddess is as bright as gold.[66] Four elephants resembling four hillocks of gold are coronating the Goddess by holding four pitchers contianing nectar with their trunks. In her four hands she holds two lotuses and shows postures of granting boons and dassurances. Her head is decked with begemmed crown, She is wearing a silk cloth and is seated on a lotus.

Each of the goddesses worshipped by the *Śāktas* has a *Yantra,* assigned to her, which is sometimes placed in the centre of a lotus-diagram. The *Śrī-cakra* is a principal *Yantra*[67] delineated in a diagram of this kind and then worshipped. It is supposed to represent the orb of the earth, nine triangles being drawn within the circle to denote the nine continents. In the centre is the drawing of a mouth, which is believed to typify the female energy (*Śakti*) presiding over the circle. According to some authorities, even the *Śaṅkarācārya was a Śakti* worshipper as he is known to have placed a representation of the Śrī C*ākra* in each of the four monastries founded by him and *Śrī Cākra* has also been described in his *Saundarya Laharī.*[68]

The *Yantras* or mystic diagrams are thought to be quite effective[69] in their operation like the *Mantras,* and of course a combination of both is held to be absclutely irresistible. Salvation and supreme felicity in a future state is obtained by drawing a six-sided or eight sided diagram and writing a particular *Mantra* underneath. Triangular, pentangular, and nine-triangled *Yantras* are equally efficacious.

Kuṇḍalinī Śaktī Yoga

According to *Śivasaṁhitā* there are four kinds of *Yoga: Mantrayoga,Haṭhayoga,* Layayoga, and *Rājyoga.*The Yoga through the rousing of *Kuṇḍalinī Śakti* is *Laya Yoga,* it means the piercing by the Kuṇḍalinī, *Śakti* of the six bodily centres or *Cakras* (also called *Padmas*-lotuses).[70]

Yoga means that process by which the human spirit (*Jivātmā*) is brought into near and constant communication with, or is merged, in the Divine Spirit (*Paramātmā*) as the nature of the human spirit is held to be separate form, (*Dvaita,* or *Visistāḍvaita*) or one with (*Advaita*) the Divine spirit. The *Śāktas* are *Advaitavādins,*[71] and according to the, identity of the two (*Jīvātmā* and Param*ātmā*) is to be realised by the Yogi.

Kuṇḍalinī, as Śabda Brahman

All the *Māntras* are supposed to be the manifestations of *Kula Kuṇḍalin,* which is a name for the *Śabda Brahman* or *Saguṇa-Brahman in* individual bodies. *Kuṇḍalinī* believed to be in the *Mūlādhāra Cakra*[72] (or basic bodily centre) is 'the cause of sweet, indistinct, and murmuring *Dhvani,* which is compared to the humming sound of a black bee. Thence *Śabda* originates and being first, i.e., *Parā* gradually manifests upwards a *Paśyanṭi, Madhyamā,* and *Vaikharī*, (the spoken speech).[73] The substance of all *Mantras,* being manifestation of *Kuṇḍalinī, is* consciousness (*cit*), manifesting as letters and words. The letters of the alphabet, are called *Akṣara* because they are the diagrammatic representation, or *Yantra* of the *Akṣara,* i.e. Imperishable *Brahman.* This is realized, however, when the *Sāāhaka's Śakti* generated by Sā*dhanā* is united with *Mantra Śakti.* The different aspects of *Devatās* as presiding deities of *Mantras* are the manifestation of the gross (*sthūla*) form of *Kuṇḍalinī,*[74] who is however extremely subtle. *"Mantra* and *Devatā* are thus one and are particular forms of *Brahman as Śiva Śakti.*[75]

Nāda-Bindu-Kalā

From the *Sakala Parameśvara,* who has been produced from *saccidānanda,* issued *Śakti*; from *Śakti* came *Nāda*;[76] and from *Nāda* issued *Bindu,* the latter being perfected out of *Ardhachandra,* issuing out of *Nāda* and becoming slightly operative towards 'speakable' (*Vacya*). The *Bindu* becomes threefold as the *Kāmakalā,* or creative will. This triangle of Divine Desire *i.e. Kāmakalā* is personified as the Great *Devī Tripura Sundarī.*[77]

Six Cakras

Out of the six bodily *cakra's*; five lower ones are situated within the spinal cord, a compound of grey and white brain nerves. *Mūlādhāra* is the lowest in the terminal, and in a midway position in the perineum between the root of the genitals and the anus. Proceeding upwards and controlling gentitals is the *Svādhishthāna,* controlling the navel region i.e. abdomen is Maṇipura, controlling the heart is *Anāhata* and controlling the throat-larynx is *Viśuddha.* Between the eyebrows is *Ājñā,* the sixth *Cakra,* and above them all in the cerebrum is *Sahasrāra,* a thousand-petalled lotus, and the highest centre of manfiestation of Consciousness in the body.[78]

These six *Cakras* or lotuses have respectively four, six, ten, twelve, sixteen and two petals which are configurations made by the position of *Yoga-Nādis* at any particular centre. These *Nādis* are not those, which are known to the *Vaidyas* or medical *śāstra, but* these are subtle channels (*Vivara*) alongwhich the *Prāṇic* current flaws.[79] The six *cakras* have their correspondences in physical body in the following nerve plexuss commencing from the lowest, the *Mùlādhāra*[80] The Sacrococcygeal plexus, the Sacral plexus, the Solar plexus (which forms the great junction of the right and left chains *Iḍā* and Pingalā with the cerebro-spinal axis) and Connected with this is the Lumbar plexus. Then follows the Cardiac plexus (*Anāhata*), Laryngeal plexus and lastly the *Ājñā* or cerebellum identified by some with the pineal Gland, the centre of the third or spritual eye. It has two lobes and above this the *Manas Cakra* or sensorium consist six, the *Soma Cakra,* the middle Cerebrum and lastly is the *Sahasrāra* the upper Cerebrum. To a great extent these localizations are yet tentative. The six *Cakras* themselves are vital centres of consciousness, within the spinal column.

Samādhi

The Practitioners of this *Yoga* hold that it is higher

than any other system and that Samādhi (ecstasy) attained thereby is more perfect. The *Samādhi* of Laya-Yoga however is said to the *Savikalpa Samādhi,* and that of *Rāja-Yoga* is *Nirvikalpa Samādhi.*[81] 'In *Mantra Yoga,* worship and devotion predominate and in the *Samādhi* of *Mantrayoga* the state of '*Mahābhāva*' is attained, marked by immobilily and Speechlessness.[82] while in *Haṭhayoga,* contemplation is made on the Light.

In *Haṭhayoga,* when *Samādhi,* called '*Mahābodha*' is attained; respiration ceases and the *Yogi* is without any sign of animation.[83] In *Layayoga the Samādhi* called '*Mahālya*' is attained; there is non outer consciousness but the *Yogi* is immersed in the Ocean of Bliss.In *Rājayoga* '*Nirvikalpa* Sam*ādhi*' is attained; there is *Nirvikalpa* or detachment (*Vairāgya*) from the world corresponding the four *yogas. The Mantra, Haṭha, Laya* and *Rāja yogas*; all these are *Mṛdu* (of high degree) and *Para* (Highest).

Mukti

Not only the *Mantra Yogi* but also the *Haṭhayogi* avails himself of the *kundalīyoga* for Liberation. The remaining two *Rājayoga* or Jñā *mayoga are termed as Dhyānayoga.*[84]

Thus there are two main lines of *Yoga,* namely *Dhyāna* or *Bhāvanāyoga and Kuṇḍalīyoga.* In *Dhyāna* yoga, sm*ādhi* is attained through detachment from the world and meditation leading to cessation of all the mental activities or the uprising of pure consciousness unhindered by the limitations of the mind[85]. This meditation is sometimes aided by auxiliary process of *Mantra or Haṭha yoga* (other than the rousing of *Kuṇḍalīni Śakti*). The degree to which the unveiling of consicousness is effected, depends upon the meditative powers (*Jñāna Śakti*) of the *Sādhaka,* and the extent of his detachment from the world[86] Here is no rousing and union of *Kuṇḍalīni Śakti* with the accompanying bliss an acquisition of special powers (*Siddhī*). In both the *yogas* bodily consciousness is lost, but there being no union of the central bodily powers with the supreme consciousness, the *Dhyānayogi* does not posses the particular kind of enjoyment (*Bhukti*). There is certainly a difference between the *Bhukti* of the *Divyayogi* and the *Vīrasādhaka*, the latter has only a refleciton of the bliss on the physical plane—a welling up of the true Bliss through the deadening coverings and trammels of matter. The so-called *Mukti* of the *Vīrasādhaka* is only figurative. It is the *Divya-yogi* only who has both, *Bhukti* and *Mukti*[87] in his hand.

Pañça-Tattvas or Makarás

Generally it is thought that in *Vāmāchāra*, woman plays an important roll. But this is only partially true in the case of those *Sādhakas*, who worship with *Śakti* according *to vāmāchāra* rites. But amongst the *Vāmāchāris* there are even *Brahmachāris*, Sādh*āka*, and followers of the *Nāthas* who never indulge in this type of *Śakti*-worhsip. *The Kālamukhas* and the *Kālavisās*, worship the *Kumāris* only upto the age of nine and the *Brahma Kaulas* refrain even from wine and meat. Now this means that this kind of worship is restricted to one section of the *Vāmāchāris*, namely the *Vīra* class[88] while the *Paśu* and *Divya* classes are prohibited performing it. There are still further restrictions that a *sādhaka* should perform this worship with his own wife, (*Svakiyā* Śakti) and it is only in the case when there is no wife that he may take some other *Śakti* for the purpose of ritual worship only.[89]

About the use of five *Makāras* in the worship, we can very well say that it is a continuation of ancient *Vedic* usage and not a modern invention. The *Tantrikas* have advanced an argument about this *Pañca Tattva Sādhanā*, that *Siddhi* can be attained by means of those very things which are the causes of men's downfall.[90] The *Tantra* says that the *Pāñcha Tattvas* are of various types, *viz*. of real (*Pratyaksha*) type, substitutional type (*Anukalpa*) and esoteric (*Divya Tattva*) type. As regards the second, even a vegetarian would not object to 'meat' which is in fact ginger and coconut water for wine.[91] As for the Esoteric *Tattvas* they are not material articles or practices, but the symbols for Yogic processes.[92] As for the first *i.e.* the real *Tattvas,* the *Tantras* contain injunctions agaist unrestrained indulgence of flesh, wine and woman.[93]

A *sāḍhaka* is to practise the seritcs, for gaining the highest object, namely the unification with *Śiva* or God, leading to emancipation. These are considered the initial steps leading towards the finalgoal. The expression Pañca Mak*āras* derives its name from the initial letters of the ingredients used in Tantric form of worship. This particular sect of the Tantrikas holds that these *Pañcā Makāras* constitute the very life of the *Tantras,* without which they cannot achieve the spiritual end.[94]

Though outwordly these rites appear much abhorent, but there is a great esoteric meaning behind these. All these, wine, meat, fish and woman are objects of temptation and it is very difficult to overcome them. Worship of a young damsel as a goddess, and taking of wine for the purpose of concentrating his mind on the object of devotion only, is something very difficult, and requires the training of the mind. The devotee here has to relinquish his own desire and self and convert the various pursuits of enioyment into instruments of spiritual discipline.

In case you have to take these in reality, the *Tantras* have prescribed the *Śodhana* ceremony which means the purification of all these five ingredients, before a devotee offers these to the deity or he partakes himself. The *Tantras* deal in detail about the purification of the *māakāras*[95] as well as of the heart of the Sādhakā. As we cannot offer anything with an impure heart to the deity, who is the object of our devotion, so we must purify everything and offer it without any selfish desire.

Esoteric meaning of the five *Makāras* is like this:—

1. *Madya*—the nectrine stream that issues from the cavity of brain, is called *Madya* or wine.[96]
2. *Mānsa*: By this term we mean the control of speech—which is only possible in case of the *Yogis.*[97]
3. *Matsya:* By fish we mean the system of respiration, drawn in and sent out. So the worshipper of fish means one who has controlled his vital breaths, this is called *Prāṇāyāmā.*[98]
4. *Mudrā:* It means the Residing place of soul in the boyd, and one who acquires the knowledge of this charming soul is he worshipper of *Mudrā.*[99]
5. *Maithuna:* the most important of all these is the practice of *Maithuna.* It is observed like thus "Cohabitation is at the root of creating, preservation and destruction: It is regarded as a great principle in scriptures and it achieves all ends and confers the most difficult knowledge of *Brahman.*[100] The meaning of *Maitnuna* here is the recitation of the various attributes of God, or unification with the God.

Thus we can say that this *Pañch-makāra* worship is not all corrupt in spirit as it is supposed to be. The object is very high and these are various instruments of spiritual disciplies.[101]

Philosophy of the Śākta Tantras

The *Śakta Tantras* hold that the Supreme Reality is *Parā* Śakti. *That* Śakti, before the manifestation of the universe and the souls, remains in a state of Quiesence or Repose, devoid as it were of the light of self-reflection implied in the nature of *Chaitanya.*[102] The unmanifest universe remains then absorbed in *Chaitanya.* This pre-creative state of Supreme *Śakti* is beyond the so-called *Parā* V*āk* of the Yogins, which is the universal Matrix and from which the Vedas and the worlds emanate.[103]

This transcendent *Śakti* is co-eternal and consubstantial with *Para Brahman* which is ineffable, indescribable, unlimited and immeasurable.[104] Only with the grace of the causal *Śakti* or mother of the worlds, this abovesaid transcendent state can be reached. Hence the *Tantras say* that every from of spiritual discipline is a sort of propitiation of the universal power.[105]

The *Parā Śakti* on this eternal plane has an eternal vision of this eternal universe, not as an object outside of itself but as its very self. This eternal vision is therefore a self-vision of *Śakti* beyond the limitations of time, space and causality and is a state of Perfect Quiet and Peace. The *Parā* Vāk or Parā is synonymous with the equilibrium of *Śiva* and *Śakti.*[106] The Supreme *Śakti,* as one with *Śiva,* transcends all *Tattvas* and as differentiated from, is the source of all *Tattvas* and is identical with them. In the later aspect it is the eternal matrix of the worlds and is of the Essence of Joy.[107]

Hence the *Śākti* has adouble aspect; and in one it is identical with *Śivā.*[108] At this stage *Śiva* alone shines. There is another aspect, in which the *Tattvas,* the universe made of the *Tattvas* and the *Devatās* appear from it, both simultaneously and successively.[109] Śaktism advocates a position intermediate between absolute monism and qualified monism. *Śiva* is the static Absolute, *Śakti* is the conscious energy of Śiva who creates the world through Sakti.[110]

Śiva and Śakti as *Brahman,* are inseparable and non - different from cach other.[111] *Śakti* is the supreme energy (*Parā* Prākṛti) *of* Śiva, the supreme self.[112] It is conscious, omniscient and the fountain head of all powers.[113] It is the source of all knowledge It is both, subtle and gross, manifest and unmanifest, formless and multiform.[114] The *Śakti* creates, preserves, and destroys the world at the mere will of *Brahman.*[115] In other words *Śiva* creates, preserves and destroys the universe through his Sakti.[116]

The *Brahman* pervades thc whole world and it depends upon him. All the things are real with the reality of *Brah-*

man. He is menifested in the world[117] and creates it through his energy (Māyā),[118] *i.e.* his *Prakṛti.* It is imbedded in *Śakti,* his supreme conscious energy. Though *Śakti* is formless, it assumes diverse forms through *Māyā.* Thus *Śaktism* combines absolute monism with the *Sānkhya* theory of evolution.[119]

The *Brahman,* however can be approached not merely as the Lord *Parameśwara,* but also as *Parameśwarī,* the Supreme *Śakti.* For she is none else but Himself in another pose. "Thou art the *Parā Praktṛti or Brāhman,* and from thee has sprung the whole universe, O *Śiva,* it is mother,"[120] She is the matrix of all that exists: Whatever there is in this world of things, with and without motion, form *Mahaṭ* to an atom, owes its origin and is dependent on thee.[121]

It is said in the *Tantras* that for the help of the worshippers, the good of the world, and the destruction of the *Dānavas,* she assumes various forms.[122] And it goes on to prescribe the best mode of worship, a swift course of *Sādhanā* for a man to effect his liberation from ignorance and achieve union with the Supreme consciousness, that is she. She manifests herself multitudiously and sports in the richness of her creation form a million centres of enjoyment. By a progressive identification of his own consciousness with larger consciousness of the world Mother, the *Sādhakā* participates in the *Līlā,* has a joy of things and in that very process of self-identification and merger grows into the nature of the Divine Mother. All the elements that make for the sustenance, growth and luxuriance of life are drawn upon in their acme and used towards this fulfilment.[123]

The Philosophy of the *Tantras* is a well-adopted reinterpretation of the doctrines, expounded by the *Upaniṣads.* The philosophy is highly monistic in tone[124] and the dual aspects of *Śiva* and *Śakti* merge ultimately in an Inscrutable unity. An identity in difference or unity in diversity has been the last word of the *Tantras.*No difference has been shown here between *Jīva* and *Śiva*. *Ātman conditioned by Upādhis or Māyā is called Jiva, but becomes Śiva,* the moment it thinks "*Sivoham*'.[125] i.e. I am *Śiva*.

Ātman is freed from those accidental attributes. In the words of Siva himself, a Śiva is entitled to eternal emanicpation when he is liberated from the bondage of *Saṁsāra*, by the force of self realisation.[126] The *Tantras* have touched the keynote of the *Avaita* philosophy by accepting identity between *Jīva* and *Brahman*, and have repeatedly stated in clear terms that the highest form of *yoga* is the attainment of unity of *Jīva* with the supreme soul.[127]

The *Tantras* have always insisted upon the supreme importance of *Jñāna*. Knowledge in its purest form is said to be the only way that leads to final emancipation. It has emphatically been asserted that *mukti* is attainable only by *Jñāa* and not by any other means.[128] The *Tantra* have only voiced the eternal truth of the Upaniṣads (न च पुनरावर्तते), when it says that Jiva once liberated is not born again.[129] Most of the *Tantras* have exalted the supremacy of *Brahmajñāna* in unequivocal terms. The *Tantras* have recognised two kinds of knowledge, one derived from the *āgamas* and the other obtained from spiritual experience.[130] The Rudrayāmala maintains that a *Tantric* worshipper ultimately becomes the same as *Brahman* through the help of *Brāma-jñānā,* and that there is no self elevating religion like *Brahman-jñānā*[131]

The *Tantras* affiliated to the *Sākta* school have explained the association of *Śakti* with *puruṣa* as the basic principle of creation. The same truth has been revealed by *Saṁkara* just in the beginning of his *Ānandalaharī.*[132]

The mysticism *of yoga,* has also been dealt with elaborately in the *Tantras*. The object of practising *Yoga,* as conceived by *Tantrikas,* is to acquire the power of visualising the Supreme Soul within the limitations of the individual soul.[133] One who longs for *mukti* is directed to think himself completely lost in all-pervading soul, and to a *yogin,* the world of perception vanishes into the absolute.[134]

Quite in agreement with the *Vedãnta* stand of point, the *Tantras* have maintained dual aspect of *Śiva*, namely *saguṇa* and *nirguṇa*. It is said further that from *saguṇa Śiva*, characterised by *sat, cit* and *ānanda*, arises *śakti* and from it evolves *nāda* and from *nāda* comes out *bindu*.The *Tantras* have shown a sublime ideal of spiritual experience which is in a sense different from all other forms of *Sādhanā*.

Last of all we can sum up that the philosophy of the *Tantras* is a reconciliation of the Absolute Monism of the *Upaniṣad's* and the dualism or qualified monism preached by some of the Purāṇas.[135]

NATURE OF THE TANTRIC SĀDHANĀ

The *Tantric Sādhanā* combines in it the elements of *Yoga,* worship, prayer and meditation on the identity of the individual & the Absolute.[136] The *Tantras* accepted the monistic philosophy of the *Upaniṣads,* appreciated the value of worship and prayer along with the *Bhakti* schools, and like the yoga system, laid great emphasis on the intimate relations between the body and the mind.[137] They preached an easy and short method of spiritual achievement, and sought to proivde persons of all grade of equipment with suitable courses of discipline.[138] The *Sādhanā* contains in it, the elements of all the important forms of *Sādhanās viz. Yoga* and *Bhakti, mantra* and *Homa,* and *Jñāna* and *Karma*.. All these when combined, go to show that the *Tantric Sādhanā*, is the synthesis of all that was good in the various forms of *Sadhanas*, and that is why its promise to its followers of the easy and speedy attainment of the end, is justified.[139] The *Tantras* promice to give to the *Sādhaka* not merely liberation (*mukti*) but also enjoyment (*bhukti*), i.e. not merely final beatitude (*Niśreyas*) but also progress (*Abhgy-udaya*)[140] in the world.

It is through the efforts of *Sādhaka* and the grace of

the spiritual guide (*Guru*) that the Serpent-power (*Kuṇḍalinī-śakti*) which generally lies dorment at the foot of the spinal column, becomes awakened and joins the Absolute, who resides in the *Sahasrāra cakra, i.e.* the highest centre of the cerebrum.[141] The word *Kuṇḍalini Śakti* is used to indicate the spiritual power of Energy of the individual human being.

The most important feature of the *Tantric Sādhanā* is that the *Tantraś* recommend the combination of *Kriyā* and *Bhāvanā* i.e. action with imagination. Here it differs with *Vedānta,* which prescribes that realisation can be had through meditation (*Bhāvanā*) alone. The *Tantras,* though declaring the unity of *jīva* and *Śiva,* differ from the *Vedānta* school, where the *Śivatva* of *jīvā* is an established fact, while according to the *Tantras, the Śivatva* (absoluteness) is to be attained through *Sādhanā.*[142]

In the *Tantras,* special importance is assigned to the *Mantras.*[143] The deity is identical with the *Mantra,* which is the infallible means of liberaiton. The *Tantras* believe in the eternity of *Mantra* and designate it as *Śabda Brahman.* The *Bīja māntras* are not mere words, but are a concentrated thought of great power, revealed to the *Sādhaka* in the hour of his profound illumination. The *Mantra Japa* is prescribed[144] for the attainment of the desired objects.

The *Tantras* lay great emphasis on *Upāsanā,* and this seems to be derived from the Purā*ṇas.*[145] The worship of the deity, and the recitation of hymans in honour of the deity, forms a very important feature in the *Tantras* as well as in the *Purāṇas.* The worshipper identifies himself in meditation, with the deity he worships[146] and places before himself the fully blossomed condition represented by the deity as the ideal to be realised. Here we see that according to the *Tantras,* the realisation of the identity between the *Jīva* and *Śiva,* is the supreme ideal.[147]

The *Tantras* recognise three distinct states of *Sādhanā*

viz. Purification (*Śuddhi*), illumination (*Sthiti*) and unification (*arpaṇa*), corresponding roughly to *Karma, Bhakti and Jñāna.*[148] The individual has to undergo various process in order to purify himself. This purification is to be attained through both, *Bhāvanā* (meditation) and *Kriyā,* and through the harmonious working of both, mind and body. The real worship of *Śiva,* is only possible by oneself, whose heart has also freed from all impurities. The last stage is of complete surrender, merging and unification. The *Jīva Śakti* is identified with *Śiva Śakti.* In this stage, no worship, and no distinction is possible but there is only Bliss, eternal and Infinite.[149]

The *Tantras* are really an epitome of all the Scriptures of the Hindus, and contain within their compass almost all the special characteristics of the various forms of *Sādhanā* if *Tantrism* prescribes actions of the most rudimentary type and seems to be very much particular about their infinite details, it again, prescribes meditation on the identity of the individual and the Absolute and thus reminds us of the high transcendent philosophy of the *Upaniṣads.*[150] It prescribes different methods and rules for the conduct of life for the persons of different equipments and capacities. It distinguishes three classes of *Sādhakas* in order of merit, viz. the *Paśu,* the *Vīra* and the *Divya.*[151] The *Paśu* is a person who has not yet attained selfcontrol but is attempting to have the mastery over his passions and impulses while the *Vīra* is a *Sādhaka* who has attained complete self-control and does not forget himself, even in the most trying and tempting circumstances. He is not only allowed, but is definitely instructed to include, such things as wine, meat, etc. as articles of offering to God,[152] while the *Paśu* is not allowed even, to touch or to have sight of those things. The method prescribed for the *Vīra* or the *Kaula* is beset with danger[153] and is more risky than the holding of a snake or clasping round the neck of a tiger. The *Divya Sādhaka* need not undergo the trials that the *Vira* has to pass through and is allowed to take substitutes of all material things in his process of worship. He does not require the help of external objects for rousing his spiritual sentiments, and the meditative mood emerges spontaneously in him. A part from this class division of the *Sādhakas, the Tantras* also mention the *kaulacāra,* which forms the highest stage, and which does away with all rules and injunctions of the *Śāstras.* For a *kaula,* there is neither any *vidhī* nor any *niṣedha,* neither merit nor demerit, and neither virtue nor sin.[154] Each *Sādhaka* have to follow his own line of development, according to his capacities and suited best to his attainments.[155]

The *Tantric Sādhanā* came into prominence perhaps later than the *Purāṇas*, although some of the *Tantras* might be dated earlier than the *Purāṇas.*The philosophy of the *Tantras* served as the basis of the *Bhakti* form of *Sādhanā,* inculcated by the *Purāṇas.*[156] There is so much similarity between the *Paurāṅika* and *Tantric* teachings that it seems unjustifiable to regard them as two distinct forms of *Sādhanā.* The union of *Śiva* and *Śakti* (God and Goddess) of the *Tantras* are also mentiond in the *Purāṇas.*[157] The eternal connection between *Śabda* and *Artha,* and the regarding of *Śabda-Brāhman* and *Pāra Brahman* as two aspects of the Supreme Lord, emphasised by the *Tantras,* finds expression in the *Purāṇas*. The doctrine of the identity of the devotee is also mentioned with the deity herself.[158] In fact the *Purāṇas* and the *Tantras* preach almost the same philosophy as well as the same method of realisation and both emphasize the importance of worship and rituals. Both these preach the cult of Bhakti and last of all their god is also the same.

Thus we see that the *Tantra* give us a synthesis between the *Upaniṣads* and the Purāṇas, by accepting the philosophy of the former and the practical *Sādhanā* of the latter.

Foot Notes

1. Woodroffe, John, *Shakti and Shata*, p.50. Kāsikā Vṛtti (7.2.9).Shukla (DN) Pratima Vijmana p. 113. Dasgupta, S.N. Philosophical Essays, p. 151.
2. Sastri H.P.—A Catalogue of Palm leaf and Selected Paper Mss.Durbar Library, Nepal, Vol. III, p. 69.
3. Kulluka Bhaṭṭa's commentary on Manusmṛti.2.1 Hārīta's words quoted by Kulluka Bhaṭṭa. Kulārṇava Tantra—2.140.
4. Bhāgavata purāṇa XI.27.7 Mahābhāgavata p. 8.77.
5. D.N.Bose and Haldar, *Tantras: their philosophy and Occult Secrets*, p. 2.
6. Brahma (N.K.), The Philosophy of Hindu Sadhana, p. 274.
7. Mahānirvaṇā Tantra, IX.13.
8. Brahma (N.K.), The Philosophy of Hindu Sadhana, p. 247-75.
9. Carl Cleman. Religions of the world, p. 12.5
10. Vārāhī Tantra: quoted by Śabda Kapadruma, Chakravarti C.,Tantras—Studies on their religion and literature, p. 2.
11. Farquhar—An Outline of the Religious Literature of India, p. 200.
12. Chakravarti, Chintaharan. The Tantras: Studies on their religion and literature, p.19.
13. Woodroffe, John. *Shakti and Shakta*,
14. Dikshitar, V.R. The Lalita Cult, p. 83
15. Mahānirvāṇā Tantra 1.16
16. D.N. Bose and Haldar, Tantras: Their Philosophy, p. 74.
17. Śakti Sangam Tantra—Kālī, Khaṇḍa, 1.22; 98.92.
18. Mahānirvāṇa Tantra, 4.10-11
19. *Ibid.* 4.35-34.
20. D.N. Bose & Haldar, Tantras, p. 86.
21. Mahānirvāṇa Tantra, 4 33-31.
22. *Ibid.* 4.35; 5.1.
23. Devī Bhāgavata 1.2.5-8
24. Prāṇatosiṇī—p. 1079
25. Šakti Sangama Tantra—Kālī Khaṇḍa 2.41; 11.

26. Mahānirvāṇa Tantra 4.10-13
27. Mahānirvāna Tantra. 4.16-18
28. Jñanārṇava Tantra—16.3-30
29. Yoginī Hṛdaya 199 p.301. Mahānirvāṇa Tantra 4.30-32.
30. Šakti Sangama Tantra—Tārā Khaṇḍa, 36.19-12.
31. Mahānirvāṇa Tantra, 4.34
32. Yoginī Hṛdaya 114, p. 228.
33. Bose ānd Haldar—The Tantras, p. 202. Alain Danielou—Hindu Polytheim, p. 273.
34. Kālī Tantra, p. 71; Mahānirvāṇa Tāntra 2.
35. Alain Danielou, Hindu Polytheism, p. 271. also Kālī Tantra quted in the aforesaid book, P. 462.
36. Šākta Pramoda, p. 27.
37. Mahānirvāṇa Tantra 4.29
38. *Ibid.* 5.137-140.
39. Kālikā UpaniŸad, 1.
40. Alain Danielou, Hindu Polytheism, p. 268
41. For names see Šabda Kalpa Druma—and Tantrasāra, two lists are these—one from Mālinivijaya and another from Mùṇœamālā Tantra. See also Šakti Sangamatantra—Sundarī Khaṇḍa 1,101-102.In this list there are some changes.
42. Alain Danielou, Hindu Polytheism p.275-277.
43. Prāṇatoṣiṇi, p. 723
44. Šākṭi Saṅgama Tantra—Kālī Khaṇḍa 2.37.39.
45. Tārā Tantra—quoted in Kalyāṇa-Šakti Aṅka, p. 224.
46. Kalyāṇa 'Šaktyaṅka', pp. 224-226.
47. Alain Danielou, Hindu Polytheism, p. 464.
48. Šākta Pramoda p. 176-178, 180-181.
49. Alain Daneilou, Hindu Polytheism. p. 279.
50. *Ibid.* p. 464. Šākta Pramoda, 203, 207
51. Bose and Haldar, The Tantras, p. 206
52. Šākta Pramoda, 260
53. *Ibid.* p. 262.
54. *Ibid.* p. 228.
55. Šākta Pramoda, p. 225.
56. *Ibid.* . 227.
57. *Ibid.* 229.
58. *Ibid.*
59. Šakti Saṅgama Tantra—Tārā Khaṇḍa, 30.23-24.
60. Toḍala Tantra, Pāâala 1.
61. Alain Danilou, Hindu Poiytheism, p. 465.
62. Šakta Pramoda, p. 281, 287-288, 290.

63. Šakti Saṅgam Tantra Tārā Khaṇḍa 30.25-26.
64. Šakta Pramoda, p. 307, 309, 310-311.
65. Ibid. p. 335, 337. Šakti Saṅgam Tantra Tārā Khaṇḍa 30.22b-23.
66. Ibid. p. 355; 357; 261. Šakti Saṅgam Tantra—Tārā Khaṇḍa 30.21-22a.
67. Alain Danielou, Hindu Polytheism, p. 359
68. Saundarya Laharī, 11. p.52. ed. Norman Brown, Harvard University Press, 1258.
69. Woodroffe, Shakti and Shakta, p. 513.
70. Šiva Saṁhitā V.14.
71. Campbell (J), Philosophies of India, p. 570.
72. Šāradā Tilaka I, p. 12. Mātṛka Bheda Tantra 3.4.
73. Yognī Hṛdaya 1.36-38; 40 Vākya Padīya-Brahma Khaṇḍa 144. Šiva Dṛshti2.1-2. Pratyabhijña Hṛdaya, 8. p. 18.
74. Prāṇa Toṣinī, p. 76, 299.
75. Jñānārṇava Tantra 13.46. John, Woodroffe, Shakti and Shakta, p. 471.
76. Jñanarnava Tantra 10.1.7. Šaradā Ṭilaka 1.7.
77. Ibid. 10.8.
78. Prāṇa Toṣinī p. 851-857. Bose and Haldar, The Tantras, p. 184.
79. Woodroffe, J.; Šakti and Šakta, p. 410.
80. *Ibid.*
81. Gheraṇḍa Saṁhitā VI.17.
82. Šakti Sangama Tantra, Kālī Khaṇḍa, 1.129-130.
83. *Ibid.* 1.121-122.
84. Mātṛka bheda Tantra 8.25-26.
85. Mahānirvāṇa Tantra 15.109-110.
86. *Ibid.* 14.112-114.
87. *Ibid.* 1.55; 4.39-43. Woodroffe—Shakti and Shakta. p. 499.
88. Mahānirvāṇa Tantra 1.57;51-56.
89. *Ibid.* 6.14. M.B. Jhaveri—Critical and Comparative Study of Mantrasāstra, p. 57-58.
90. Kulārṇava Tantra V.68.
91. Šakti Sangama Tantra——Kālī Khandạ 9.16-33.
92. *Ibid.* 9.16-17. Prāṇatoṣinī, p. 1049.
93. Kulārṇava Tantra : 2.117-18. Mahānirvāṇa Tantra 6.13-16. Prāṇā Toṣini, p. 1050.
94. Šakti Sangama Tantra, Kālī Khanda 9.18.

95. Prāṇa Toṣinī Tantra p. 1042. Mahānirvāṇ Tantra 6.1-16.
96. Prāṇa Toṣinī Tantra, p. 1041.
97. Ibid. p. 1042. Āgama Sāra.Chakaravarti, C. The Tantras, p. 41.
98. Āgama Sāra. 99. Ibid.
100. Prāṇa Toṣinī Tantra, p. 1343. Diskshitar. Lalita Cult p. 79.
101. Ibid. p. 982 Chakravarti (C), The Tantras Studies of their religion and literature. p. 42.
102. Saraswatī Bhawan Studies, Vol. X, p. 22.
103. Vākyapadīya of Bhartûhari, p. 1-6 Part I, Brahmakaṇœa.
104. Mahānirvāṇa Tantra, 3.6.-9.
105. Saraswatī Bhawan Studies, Vol. X, p. 23.
106. Prapañcasāra Tantra 2.43 Brahma (N.K.), Ibid p. 286.
107. Šakti Sangama Tantra; Kālīkhaṇœa 1.98-99
108. *Ibid.* 1.102-103
109. Saraswati Bhavan Studies, Vol. x, p. 29. Šakti Sangama Tantra, Kālīkhaṇœa, 1.112-116.
110. Mahānirvāṇa Tantra 4 10. K, 25-29.
111. Šakti Samgam Tantra, Kali Khanda, 2.11
112. Mahā Nirvāṇa Tantra 4 10
113. *Ibid.* 4.14
114. *Ibid.* 5.10-15, Kālī Tantra 9.22.
115. Māhā Nirvāṇa Tantra 4.30-34.
116. *Ibid.* 4.23-27. 117. *Ibid.* 5.195.
118. *Ibid.* 14.127; 4.34; 5.19.
119. Sinha (J.N.) A History of Indian Philosophy, Vol. II. p.746.
120. Mahānirvāṇa Tantra 4.10
121. *Ibid.* 4.11 122. *Ibid.* 4.15-16.
123. Prandit (M.P.), Studies in the Tantras and the Veda, p. 21-29.
124. Brahma (N.K.), Philosophy of Hindu Sadhana p. 292.
125. Kulārṇava Tantra, 9.42
126. *Ibid.* 14.7
127. *Ibid.* 9.30 Šakti Sangam Tantra, Kālī Khaṇḍa 1.117.
128. Kularāṇava Tantra 1.105.
129. Tantrarāja Tantras 36.

130. Kulārṇava Tantra 1.109 131. Rudra Yāmala Tantra.
132. Ānandalaharī—1. 133. Kulārṇava Tantra 9.30.
134. Šakti Sangama Tantra, Kālī Khaṇḍa 1.130.
135. Brahma (N.K.), Philosophy of Hindu Sādhanā, p. 275.
136. Šakti Sangama Tantra 1.56.
137. Brahma (N.K.), Philosophy of Hindu Sādhanā, p. 83.
138. Mahānirvāṇa Tantra, 2.20-22.
139. Kulārṇava Tantra 2.21; 36.
140. Ibid 3.96
141. Brahma (N.K.), Philosophy of Hindu Sādhanā, p. 277. See also footnote No. 8.
142. Kulārṇava tantra 9.43
143. Brahma (N.K.) Philosophy of Hindu Sādhanā, p. 278.
144. Mahānirvāṇa Tantra 5.83
145. Brahma (N.K.), Philosophy of Hindu Sādhanā, p. 278.
146. Gandharva Tantra 8 1. Šakti Sangam Tantra, Kālī Khaṇḍa, 8.22.
147. Kālikopaniṣad. Šakti Sangam Tantra—Kālī Khaṇḍa, 1.130-131.
148. Brahma (N.K.), Philosophy of Hindu Sādhanā, p. 280. Mātṛka Bheda Tanta 12.44; 3.39
149. Šakti Sangam Tantra—Sundarī Khaṇda, 2.186-137.
150. Brahma (T.K.), Philosophy of Hindu Sādhanā, p. 290.
151. Mahānirvāṇa Tantra 1-51-53.
152. *Ibid.* 1.57.
153. Kulārṇava, 2.122.
154. Mahānirvāṇa Tantra 4.36-45.
155. Mātṛka Bheda Tantra 14.3-10
156. Brahma (T.K.), Philosophy of Hindu Sādhanā, p. 81
157. Šakti Sangama Tantra—Sundarī Khaṇḍa 4.55. Devī Bh. 7.15-16.
158. Kulārṇava, Tantra, 9.42.

Three

Ritualistic Aspect of the Purāṇic Śakti-Cult

The Vedas as an Authority of Dharma

The *Śākta Purāṇas* hold the Vedas in high esteem in the matters of Sadācara and the *ceremonies*; and try its best to establish their authority among the people.[1] Devi Bhāgavata calls it '*Veda Saṁhitā*' *and* claims to contain the essence of the Vedas. It regards *Śruti, Smṛti* and *Purāṇa* as sources of *Dharma* and looks upon the first as the highest authority.[2]

It says that '*Śruti*' *and* '*Smṛit*' are regarded as the two eyes, and the Purāṇas as the heart. The Presentations of these three only should be taken as *Dharma* and in case of disagreement among these three, *Śruti* is the determining authority.[3] In the *Purāṇas* there are certain matters, though derived from the *Tantras,* regarded as *Dharma*, but one must not follow them blindly. If the *Tantra* does not go against the *Veda*, it is to be regarded as an authority, if otherwise, then it should not be considered authority on *Dharma*. Every *Śāstra*, be it *Smṛti,* Purāṇa, *Tantra* or any thing else, should be regarded as authoritative, in case it is based on the Veda, and never otherwise.[4] All those people viz. the followers of *Kāmācara Pāśupata*, *Linga Dhārin* and the *Vaikhānasa* schools, fare outside the pale of the *Vedic Dharma* and it is said that they all go to hell.[5]

While discussing the ritualistic aspect of the *Purāṇic Śakti* cult, we have to bear in mind that it is of puritan style. The worship consists of *Pujā,* donations, sacrifices *Vratas*, meditation and pilgrimages to *Śakti Pithās.*[6] The *Pūja* is of two types, one performed by the individuals[7] and second by the community. The large functions were arranged to perform community *Pujā,* like *Durgā pujā* in *Navarātara, Ambā Yajñā* and Ratha yātrā fair.[8] For an individual *Sādhaka,* the *purāṇas*, specifieally prescribe the codes of *Sadācāra.* It is said that a man devoid of good character is always a failure in this world and after-wards.[9] *Sadācāra* is very much praised in the *Purāṇas.*

To honour the authority of the *Vedas,* the *Śākta Purāṇas* even prescribe the *Japa of Gāyatrī Mantra, a Vedic Mantra.*[10] In the performance of the rites and *Homa*, so many *Vedic Mantras* are utilised, and a great respect is shown towards the *Brāhmines,*[11] who are called *Śāktas*, due to their observances of *Vedic* rites.

Śaktism—As a sect

Devī Bhagavata Purāṇa mentions many times the different cults of Hinduism prevalent in that period.[12] While it mentions *Yogis, Vānaprasthis*, ritualists, *Dixits*, performing *Tapas*, devotees of *Śiva*, *Ganeśa*, *Sun Viṣṇu* and many others. Mention has also been made of the *Śaktas*—as an important cult of India, (as it has been indicated by its inclusion in the list just after (*Śaivas*). *Śakti* at that time was considered as one of the five (*Panchayatāna*) deities *viz. Śiva, Śakti, Ganeśa*, Sun And *Viṣṇu.*[13]

Śakti-worship was prevalent among the *kirātas.*[14] Like other cults—Śaktism also included the *Śudras, Mlechas, Yavanas, Vrātyas*, ladies, married-unmarried or widowed—as their sectaries.[15]

Sometimes the opposition was also there of the cult of *Sakti* by the votaries of other sects.[16] It is said that *Sīddha-yogīsvara*, not worshipping *Śakti* had fallen from his elevated position. The *Purāṇas* give a long list of devotees of *Śakti* which are generally the kings, or the celebrated personalities of Hindu mythology or history Besides these the people in general were also devoted to the goddess.[17]

Adhikāris of Devī-worship

The Śakta Purāṇas hold a liberal view about the position of women and the Sudras, and allowed to perform the worship of Devī. It allows them as well as the *Pukvāsas*, *Candālas* and others to perform the vows and worships connected with Devī,[18] and even prefers a qualified *Śudra* to a worthless member of any of the higher castes.[19] Women and *Śudras* are directed to perform *homa* daily in a sanctuary (*Math*) or a kitchen (*Mahānasa*) but never in a *Kuṇḍa*.[20]

A man who is well-versed in *Devī Śāstras* and has knowledge of the *Mātṛ Maṇḍala* though he may not be a *Naiṣṭhika Brahmachāri*, is eligible for performing *Devī*-worship no matter whether he is a *Brāhman*, or a *Kshatriya*, or a *Vaiśya* or a *Śudra*. A *Devī*-worshipper is to worship *Śakti* according to the prescribed formula and not otherwise.[21] The person knowing *Devi śāstras* is honoured and respected by everybody.[22]

About the *ugra* form of *Devī*, it is said in the *Purāṇas* and also generally believed that the devotee of the goddess should have a strong heart, and while looking towards the fearful appearance of *Devī*, he should not be frightened. If he is successful in such a test put by the goddess herself, he is rewarded by her grace, gets all the things desired and help from the goddess. If otherwise, he may be punished,[23] even upto the extent of mental derangement.

Devī Pūjā

By the study of the *Purāṇas,* it known that the goddess was generally worshipped on the banks of the rivers, ocean, or tanks, and people ordinarily constructed *Devī Pratimās* of the clay.[24] In the *Purāṇas* only *Daksiṇa Mārga* was followed, which means that vegetarian way of worship was preferred though cases of the offering of one's own blood have been enumerated. Human sacrifice was condemned and even the offering of the animals is not welcomed at least by *Brahmins.*

It is said that if a devotee worships Devī with a particular object in his mind, he gets the fulfillment of that object as well as the final salvation in the end, as a result of that worship.[25] The Media of worship of the different goddesses are usually *Pratima* (image in a temple), *Maṇḍal, Yantra, Linga, Ghaṭa* (pot), *Pustaka, Pādukā,* Sword, and *Chitra* etc.[26] A newly constructed image was first to be infused with life (*Prāṇa Pratiṣṭhā*) to confer divinity on it.[27]

Places for Worship

The different places are mentioned for Devī worship. *Devī Purāṇa* says that the goddess was worshipped in the cities, villages, towns, localities, in the temples, on the bank of the river, under the tree, on the top of the mountains, in the forest, in the houses, at the cross roads, on the gates of cities, forts or houses, on the bank of the river Ganges, *Vindhya* mountains, *Veda Parvata, Śrisaila, Kiskindhā Parvata* etc., varying according to the circumstances, mean and different purposes.[28] Though these places, certainly render immediate results if *Śakti* is properly worshipped, but she may be worshipped anywhere else and the place will be called *Śakti Peetha.*[29]

Time and days for Worship

Devī or mother goddesses are to be worshipped especially at a time when the sun remains in the *Kanyā Raśi,*[30] or in the evening. After worship lamps, full of *Ghee* may be offered. At the time of difficulties in the country, *Devis* are to be worshipped in the *Giri Durga.*[31] She is generaly worshipped on *Mahānavamī, or Mahāṣṭami, Purṇamāsī, the Aṣṭamis* of every month, and Night of the *Divāli* day. The days preferred for worship are Tuesday and saturday.[32] *Navarātra* worship is to be celebrated compulasrily both by the individuals in their houses and collectively in the public places—like temples, banks of the rivers and celebrated *Śakti-Peethās.*[33]

The word worship is designated by various names—*Pujā, Archanā, Saparyā, and Bhajana.*[34] The *Pūjā* falls under the *Kāmya* sacrifices. In a *Pūja* ceremony the most important thing is that there should be something representing the object of worship, called *Pratīka or Pratimā,* for external (*Bāhya*) *Pūjā* and for Mental worship the mental image is required.[35] The worship is accompanied with elaborate rituals and ceremonies[36] and these rituals in the *Purāṇas* are different from the *Tantric* ones, as far as their aims and objects are concerned. In their nature also, these are not so complicated, mystical and mysterious ones as the rituals of the *Tantras* are Here *Bali* and *Homa* are prescribed in every *Pujā* and *Yoga* is also given due place in *Śakti* worship. Music and dancing form an integral part of the worship. Idol-worship in the temples forms an important part of *Śaktism.*[37] The image of Devi may also be worshipped in the houses and for the worship of an idol sixteen *Upacāras* are considered essential. The *Purāṇas* give in detail the steps of worship and these are given below in brief.

Upaçāras

The *Upacarās* are consisting of the materials used or things done. These are generally sixteen: (1) *Āsana* (seating of the image); (2) *Svāgata* (welcoming of the *Devata*);

(3) *Pādya* (water for washing the feet); (4) *Arghya* (offerings which may be general or *sāmānya* and special or *Viśeṣa*) made in the vessels; (5) *Ācamana* (water for sipping and cleansing the lips is offered twice); (6)*Madhuparka* (honey, ghee, milk and curd); (7) *Snāna* (water for bathing); (8)*Vasana* (cloth or garment); (2) investing it with a sacrificial string; (*Yajnopavita*) (1) *Añbharaṇa* (jewels), (11) *Gandha* (perfume); (12) *Puṣpa* (flowers); (13) *Dhūpa* (incense); (14) *Dīpa* (light); (15) *Naivedya* (food); and (16) *Vandana or Namaskriyā* (prayer)[38] and last of all *Dakshina.*

The *Purāṇas* and other works give various details in connection with the particular articles to be offered to a particular deity, e.g. the *Bel* or *Bilva* leaves and *Kalhāra* flowers to *Śiva*; the *Tulasi* leaf to *Viṣṇu,* the scarlet hibiscus (*Javā*) to the Goddess, etc. The *Mantras* may also vary according to the deity to be worshipped.[39]

In the beginning of a worship, the welcoming (*āvāhana*) and life-giving (*prāṇa-pratiāṣṭhā*) ceremonies of a deity, and at the conclusion, the act of the bidding of the deity (to depart) (*visarjana*) are essential.

Mantras

Devi *Bhāgavata* mentions three *Mantras of Devī.* viz. *Vāg Bāja, Kāma Bīja* and *Māyā Bījā,* the seed *Mantras of Vāk, Kāma and Māyā.*[40] The *Kāma Bīja* is called the king of the *Mantras* and the persons meditating on that, cannot be overpowered even by gods.[41] *Kālikā Purāṇa* mentions the *Mantras* or *Gāyatris* of every goddess. *Gāyatri Mantra* is considered a sacred *Mantra*. Besides these three *Mantra,* there are other Mantras[42] which are used in the worship of *devī* and in the sacrifices like *Ambā Yajña* or *Navārātra* cermony.

Nāmajapa

It is also an important feature in the worship and the

Various names of Devi are to be recited. For that purpose the authors of the *Purāṇas* have given various *Sahasranāmas* to be read on sacred occasions[43] and besides these one thousand names of the goddess, we get the long lists of her names in the various *Purāṇas*. It is always maintained that *Nāmajapa* is a very meritorious act.[44]

SACRAMENTAL MEALS OR FEASTS

The sacrificial offerings are closely associated with sacramental meals. The primary notion of the offering, is a gift to the gods; it is mostly a food. It was the custom that some portion of the offering was consumed by the priests or the worshippers. The sacramental meal is obviously a joyous celebration.[45] When partaking in such a community meal celebration, the worshipper felt himself released from the displeasure of the god and goddess and he also felt renewed friendly relations with the worshipped. But these meals have another deeper significance *i.e.* the communion with the deity here assumes more intimate and mystical form,[46] the idea in the minds of the people, though varying due to time and place, is that by participation in these sacramental meals, the qualities and powers of the deity are assimilated in the human body. The *Purāṇas* dealing with *Śakti*-worship associate with every occasion of worship, the sacramental meals. First of all, *Brāhmiṇs* and *Kumāris* should be fed and then the relatives and others present there, as well as the devoteet themselves take part in these ceremonial feasts.[47]

YEALRY-WORSHIP

Devī is worshipped in all the 12 months and different articles are offered to her. The names of the goddess are also different from month to month.[48]

1.	*Mārga Śiras*	Rasa
2.	*Pauṣa*	Ghee, & a cow made of Ghee.
3.	*Māgha*	Tila.

4.	*Phālguṇa*	Food-grains
5	*Chaitra*	Clothes
6	*Vaiśākha*	Barley, Wheat
7.	*Jyeṣṭhā*	Clay pitcher full of water
8.	Āshāḍha	Chandan, Karpūra
9.	*Shrāvana*	Butter
10.	*Bhādrapada*	Umbrella
11.	*Aśvina*	Gur, Sugar
12.	*Kārtika*	*Dīpa dāna*

and the cow made of gold may be given in all months.

Articles used in Worship

The Purāṇas generally prefer to have all the vegetarian articles to be used in the worship of *Śakti.*[49] Though instances are there when we see that meat and wine are offered to Devi,[50] but *Devī Bhāgavata Purāṇa* Justifies it by saying that, if a devotee is habituated to take these, then only he should offer these to the goddess. The *Purāṇas* enlist the following things to be used in her worship and offered in *Naivaidya*[51] such as water, milk, *Bilva Patra, Pāyas, Dhūpa, Gandha, Kumkuma,* flowers, fruits, *ghee,* Mangoes, Sugar, Tila, Camphor, rows of lamps, *Candan,* Sweatmeats, rice, *Guda,* Sugarcane, oil of *Tila,* preparation of barley, *Indu* flowers, red lotuses, garland of flowers, *Ghantā, Cāmara, Yantra,* Silken clothes, ornaments, book, *Kambala,* red clothes, red flowers, and all other things, offered to her with devotion and *Śraddhā.*[52] Having performed *Pujā* In this way and having offered the *Naivaidya* to the goddess, one may perform other sacrifices. The worship gives to a devotee the desired objects and salvation. Now we discuss the othe rites of *Śakti*-cult.

Devī Pratimā Swarupa

An image of *Devī* may be made in accordance of all the *Lakshṇas,*[53] *Pratima* should be decorated with all the ornaments, *Mukut* on her head made of jewels, large ears and eyes, Her face shining with lustre, like lightening, having *Mālā or* bracelet; around the neck, blossoming breasts, three lines on the belly, bit *Nitamabas*; having big and fleshy thighs, feet along with *Nupuras,* hands having *Keyūra,* also having three yes, and clad in yellow garments. She should be depicted either mounting on lion, or sitting on throne. She should be in a pose of destroying the demons and enemies, and she may be depicted either with ten arms or twenty arms.[54]

1. Two hands—holding in one, *Aksh* and in the second *Danda.*
2. 28 hands—holding sword,[55] *Khetaka, Gada,* Rod, Arrow, Bow, *Hala, Mūsala, Pāśa, Tomara, Ḍhakkā, Paṇava, Tanjanam Svastika, Abhaya, Aksha, Mudgara, Paraśu, Cakra, Damaru,* Mirror, *Śakti, Kuntas, Nāgapāśa Naramunḍa Danḍa, making noice, and killing the enemies.*

Materials for Devī images

The images of Divine is made of different materials[56] viz. Gold,[57] precious stones, marvel, clay,[58] Metal picture, and wood etc.[59] varying according to the different objects to be achieved

Devī Purāṇa mentions that the images of the goddess are made of stone,[60] of *Indra-Nīla-Maṇi,* of gold, of silver, of brass, of *Muktāphala,*of food grain (flour), of copper,, of *Sphaṭika Mani,* of blue suffire, of steel, and *Mantramayī* as well as of mind *i.e.* mental images made of Devi.[61] By worshipping the goddess in different images of different metals the person may obtain different results. By worshipping the images of stone—*Indra-nīlamani,* gold, silver, brass, *Kāmikā,* clay, *sphaṭika,* of flour, copper, *Muktāphala, Pravālaka* or iron—the results to be attained are, destructive power, lord of wealth, fame, movement, beautiful body, wealth, charming personality, overwhelming lustre, luxuries, motherhood etc. respectively.[62] *Devī Bhāgavata* mentions only *Mṛnmayī Pratimā* for all sorts of objects to be achieved.

Devi Sthāpanā Phala

Installation of *Devī Pratimā* or construction of a *Devī* temple on the bank of river *Gangā* and *Narmadā,* or on the top and in the vicinity of *Vindhya, Arbuda, Himālaya* mountains, or on the banks of rivers, in the forts, in lanes, at the crossroads, and in the forests, gives all success to the devotees.[63]

2. By the installation of Devi image in cemetry grounds, our enemies are destroyed.[64]
3. Installation in *Ekalinga,* tree, mountain, house, place for cattle, gives happienss and health.[65]
4. Installation in all the places, gives *Mokṣa.*[66]
5. Installation on *Navamī* of *Āśvina,* of the image made of clay even gives all success.[67]

Goddess being pleased by devotion and worship gives all happiness in the life and salvation in the end.[68]

Temples

In the *Purānas*[69] there are references of *Devī* templeṣ A temple is mentioned amidst the *Vindhya* range.[70] A tample constructed by a devotee, must be furnished with all the upakarnas, and the outlook should be very good. It should be possessed of *Gantā,* banner, umbrella, towers, tent and mirrors. It may be having all the musical instruments and the orchestra playing daily there. The learned persons should be welcomed there.[71] Whosoever, dedicates this type of temple to Devī, enjoys the world and goes to *Devī Loka,* and his predecessors as well as the successors are also upraised.[72]

Very Good results can be obtained by constructing the new temples, as well as by overhauling the old ones. Even the images of the goddess are to be changed along with full details of the *Prana Prāṇtiṣṭhā* ceremony.[73]

Donations

Each and everything, obtained in right way may be

donated in honour of Devī. Even the vegetables and nonvegetables may be offered in donation to the virgin girls, or ladies, *Brāhmines* or devotees of Devī,[74] and the Goddess is highly pleased by such donations it is said.

1. The list of articles to be donated is like thus: Land, gold, cows, paddy, *Tila,* clothes and *Ghee,* etc. all the things, which are necessary for life.[75]
2. The places where the donations may be made[76] are enumerated viz. *Vārāṇasi, Gayā, Vindhyas*, bank of the river *ganges,*temples of *Devī* and *Pithas* of *Śakti* and all other places.

Agnisthāpna

Maintenance of the sacred fire, was a duty of those, who are well-versed in the literatures of the *Vāmās* and the *Dakshinās* as well as in *Vedānta* etc.[77] Homa was permitted to be performed by the members of the higher castes as well as by the *Śudras,* women and children.[78] *Agni* in *Devī Purāṇa* is having three names—*Agni, Hutāśan,* and *Anala* and it is said that the gods reside in these fires.[79]

Viḍyādāna

It is considered very meritable act to donate *Vidyā. Devī* is to be worshipped at this occasion with great devotion by the donator.

First of all, the book is worshipped with flowers and other things; and honour is bestowed to the author, who is *Śāstra Pāraga.* The *Mātṛs* and other gods and goddesses are also worshipped on this occasion. Then the manuscript is taken in a car to a temple of *Śiva* or *Devī,* and is given to a learned teacher or a *Brāhman.*[80]

Vasudhārā

It is a name given to the performance of *Homa* with the pouring of *Ghee* in the fire.[81] *Devī Purāṇa* mentions the different results by pouring *Ghee* into the fire by the people belonging to different castes and on different days specially on *Sankrānti* days.[82] It is said that goddess, satisfied with this *Homa* fulfils all the desires of a person.[83] Specially the kings are required to perform this *Homa* called *Vasudhārā* according to their own means for their own welfare as well as for the betterment of the country.[84] The *Havana* may be performed in the *Kuṇḍas,* made of gold or silver or brass metals,[85] although *Ghee* and other things like milk, juice, grains, seasams, rice and *Kuśa* may be poured in the fire.[86] Different types of *Man tras* are given to perform different steps in the ceremony and *Vaidika Mantras* are generally preferred. But instructions are also there to choose *Mantra* from *Atharvaveda* only.[87] In the end a *Stuti* is to be made either of *Devī* or of *Agni.*

This home is to be performed by every one, without any distinction of caste. But the *Purāṇa* perscribes that the following qualities must be possessed by a person. He must be self controlling; taking balanced food, well-versed in all the lores, habituated to perform *Japa* and *Homa.* He should abstinate from speaking with crooked and deformed persons and others.[88]

Generally the *Homa* may be performed daily, unless there is some extra-ordinary troubles caused either by the lack of money, or shortage of *Ghee*, or revolt in the state and some dacoity takes place.[89] *Devi Purāṇa* gives a list of important and significant days when this *Vasudhāra* should be performed for the betterment by the individuals, and for the prosperity and uplift of the masses—by the king.[90] These days are:—the 8th and the 9th day of bright half of *Āsvina,* called *Mahāṣṭamī* and *Mahānavami,*[91] the full-moon day of *Kārtika*, *Vaiśākha* and *Jyaiṣṭha,* 12th day of *Āṣḍāha,* and 8th and full moon day, and days of eclipses and so on.[92]

Ambā Makha

In the second book of *Devī Bhāgavata* there is a mention

of *Devi Makha*. It is advised there by the sage *Uttanka,* well versed in the *Tantric* cult, to the king *Janmejaya,* that you perform *Sarpa Yaṅa* under the pretext of *Ambā Makha.*[93]

There is also mention of the world *Devī Yajña Vidhāna,*[94] which shows that till the time of the composition of this *Purāṇa,* the texts dealing with ritualistic details have been composed and the cult was in its full swing during this period. It is said that *Indra* performed this *Yajña* and also King *Nimi* made preparations for that.[95] *Viṣṇu* also performed *Devi Yajña* for the sake of creation and last of all king *Janmejaya,* the great grandson of the *Pāṇḍavas,* performed it with great devotion[96] and with great pump and show.

Rathayātrā Mahotsava

Though there are references of *Rathayātrā* of *Devī* in the other *Purāṇas,* but it is the *Devī Purāṇa* only which gives full detail of the celebrations.[97] It is celebrated with great enthusiasm and with pump and show. People gather together and take part in the function, and having worshipped the car, made of gold and jewel etc., covered with silk—bedecked with *Ghantā, Chamar, Patakā* and flag,[98] and Devi is placed on the car and worshipped, reciting the name's of *Durgā, Kātyāyanī,* Varada, *Vindhya-Vāsinī*; *Umā,* beloved of *Śiva*; *Mātā*; *Nisumbha-Sumbha Mathini Mahishāsurā-Kshayankarī*; and *Sarva-mangala-Mahgalā.*[99] *Devī Purāṇa* says that on the prescribed dates *viz.* fifth, seventh ninth, and eleventh, *pujā* is performed first and having offered the *Bali* to the goddess, *Devī* is placed in a car. A *Manḍapa* of stone or clay may be constructed[100] at the mountains at the banks of river, and *Sangam* of rivers. After placing the image of the goddess in a *Ratha*, procession should proceed toward the *Manḍapa*. The procession is consisted of the people, ladies and children, and possessed of food, water, and the large number of *Naivaidyas* etc.; and while moving, *Bali,* may be offered to *Bhūtas* and *Pretas*[101] along with the recitation of *Mantras.*

Then reaching to the fixed place, taken down the image of *Devī* from car and place it on a platform, made inside the *Madapa*; *Diva* is to be bathed with water poured from the new *Kalaśas,* made of gold, silver or copper, full of ausp cious leaves and fruits along with the recitation of the *Vedic Mantras* and with music, vocal and instrumental.[102] Then follow the usual steps viz. *Pūjā* of *Devī,* feeding of *Kanyās, Brāhmins,* other poor fellows and relatives.

After this, *Devī* is to be placed on car again to bring her back, and followed, by, a huge crowed.[103] The whole route of the procession should be well-decorated. Women are to utter auspicious words and scatter flowers, *Dūrvā,* and rice etc.,[104] On this occasion each and every house in the city should be decorated and cleansesd properly.[105] On this event of happiness and festivity, no tree should be cut down, no killing of the animlasor of human beings, the prisoners may be released from the prison and one should try to control anger.[106] The Gods, *Yakshas, Kinnaras* enjoy the heavenly life by performing this festival, performed with great festivity.[107]

Dhvajadānam

Devi Purana says that the *Dhvajas* (banners) may be made of cloth, and their stick map be of gold, wood, stone, etc. and having the emblem of lion or any other *Vāhana* on it, may be prepared and the temples be furnished with these flags and donated in the end[108] This ceremony was called *Dhvajdāna* ceremony,[109] having the following constituents.

1. Performance of *Homa.*
2. *Devī,* worship, according to one's own means on *Navamī* [110] day.
3. Feeding of the girls and the *Brāhmins*

4. Offering of food to the beings.[111]
5. Devotee has to observe certain discipunes such as Upavāsa[112] and should be pure, alert, and no contact with the bad people.
6. Welcoming the *Bhaktas* of *Devī.*[113]
7. With the recitation of *Mantras,* banners were installed on the top of the temples.[114]
8. Aims—It beautifies the temples, fulfils all the desire. If king takes the banner in his hand he will be victorious in the battle and all the troubles are removed.[115]

Kumārī Pūjā

It is only those girls who are healthy, graceful, beautiful, without any ulcers, and who are not bastards; these virgins, are to be selected for *Kumārī Pūjā.*[116] And the girls, who are defective in limbs, lepers, with ulcers, of offensive smell or whose bodies are polluted, born in a bad family, blind, squint eyed, of disgraceful appearance whose bodies are over grown with hairs, who are diseased, are in their menstruation period, of passionate nature, very lean and thin, or born of widows, or of woman unmarried, are not to be accepted for *Kumārī pūjā.*[117]

In all the cases, the *Kumārīs,* born of the *Brāhmin* families can be worshipped; when victory is desired, the *Ksatriya Kumāris* are preferred; when money is desired, the *Vaiśya Kumāris*; when general welfare is wanted, the *Śudra Kumāris* are to be worshipped.[118] In the *Navarāṭra Pujā,* the *Brāhmins* should select for worship only the *Brāhman Kumāris*; the *Ksatriyas* should select *Brāhmant* or *Ksatriya* and the *Vaisya* worshippers can select *Brāhmana Ksatriya* or *Vaiśya Kumārīs*. And in case of *Śudra* worshippers there is no restrictions and he can select a *Kumāri,* from any of the four classes.[119] But artists and artisans should select the *Kumāris* from their own families and tribes respectively.[120]

In *Navarātra Pujana* the worship of *Kumāris* is an

important item.[121] Everyday, during the *Navarātara* the devotee is asked to worship *Kumāris* ranging from the age of two years to the age of ten. Not more than nine kumaris, according to the number of *Tihtis*, are to be worshipped.[122] These nine virgin girls are named thus respectively, *Kumārikā; Trimurti, Kalyānī, Roṇiṇī, Kālikā, Candikā, Śāmbhavī, Durgā* and *Subhadrā*.[123] The girls aged below one year and more than ten years are not to be included in *Kanyāpūjan*,[124] Different results are said to be obtained by the worship of the girls belonging to the different age groups.

1. *Kumārī:* The worship of *Kumārī* (of the age of two years) leads to the extinction of miseries and poverty, to the exserpation of one's enemies and the increment of riches, longevity and power.[125]

मन्त्र कुमारस्य च तत्वानि या सृजत्यपि लीलया।
कादीनपि च देवांस्तान् कुमारीं पूजयाम्यहम्।।

2. *Trimurtī*: *Pujā of Trimurtī* yields longevity, and the acquisition of the first three aims of life, viz. *Dharma,* wealth (Artha), and desires (Kāma), as well as the rewards with the riches, son and grandsons.[126]

मन्त्र—सत्वादिभिस्त्रिमूर्तिभिर्यातैर्हि नानास्वरूपिणी।
त्रिकालव्यापिनी शक्तिस्त्रिमूर्तिपूजयाम्यहम्।।

3. Kalyaṇī: Those who want learning, victory, kingdom, and happienss, they should worship the kumari named *Kalyāṇī,* the fructifier of all desires.[127]

मन्त्र—कल्यारगाकारिणी नित्यं भक्तानां पूजितानिशम्।
पुजयामि च तां भक्त्या कल्याणीं सर्वकामदाम्।।

4. *Rohiṇī:* She should be worshipped by the people duly with devotions for the cure of diseases.[128]

मन्त्र—रोहयन्ती च बीजानि पूर्वजन्मसंचितानि च।
या देवी सर्वभूतानां रोहिणीं पूजयाम्यहम्।।

5. *Kālikā*: For the destruction of the enemies, the worshipped of *Kālikā* with due devotion, is considered the best.[129]

मन्त्र—काली कालयते सर्व ब्रह्मांडं सचराचरम्।

कल्पान्तसमये या च तां कालिकां पूजयाभ्यहम्।।

6. *Candikā: Candikā* is to be worshipped with devotion by the devotees[130] or prosperity and riches.

मन्त्र—तां चंड पापहारिणीं चंडिकां पूजयाभ्यहम्।

7. *Śāmbhavī*: For the enchanting and over-powering of one's enemies, for the removal of miseries and poverty and for the victory in the battles, worship of *Śāmbhavi* is said to be the only means.[131]

मन्त्र—अकारणात्समुत्पतिर्यन्मयैः परिकीर्तिता।
यस्यास्तां सुखदां देवीं शांभवीं पूजयाभ्यहम्।।

8. *Durgā:* For the destruction of awfully terrible enemies and for the happiness in the next world, the worship of *Durgā* is called the safest and the best.[132]

मन्त्र—दुर्गात् त्रायति भक्तं या सदा दुर्गतिनाशिनी।
दुर्ज्ञेया सर्वदेवानां ता दुर्गा पूजयाभ्यहम्।।

9. *Subhadrā:* People worship *Subhadra* and all their desires are fulfilled and ill luck is removed.[133]

मन्त्र—सुभद्रारिणी च भक्तानां कुरूते पूजिता सदा।
अभद्रनाशिनीं देवीं सुभद्रां पूजयाम्यहम्।।

People should worship the *Kumāris* with the *Mantras*, beginning with *Śrī* or with the seed *Mantras* and giving them clothings, ornaments, garlands, scents and various other articles.[134] Thus by prescribing the worship of the girls and the ladies *Śaktism* tried to raise the social status of the womanhood in the society. The *Purāṇas* maintain that a girl or a lady is either her miniature incarnation or the goddess herself.[135]

Durgā-Pujā in the Navarātras

From the first day of *Āsvina* shukla to the 9th, is celebrated the *Durgā Pūjā* festival, called *Navarātra*, and it is observed all over India in some form or other.[136] Though there are two *Navarātras*, falling, one in *Caitra* and another in *Āsvina*,[137] but it is specially the *Navarātra* of autumn season, the *Durgāpūjā* is celebrated in a grand style.[138] The *Purāṇas* and the *Upapurāṇas* deal in detail with *Durgā-pūjā* in the Navaratras in the month of *Āsvina.*[139]

Objects: The *Pujā* is *Nitya* as well as *Kāmya.* The *Kālikā Purāṇa* says that whoever, thorugh laziness, hatred or stupidity, does not celebrate the great festival of *Durgā,*has all his derires frustrated by the anger of *Devī.*[140] It is *Kāmya* because rewards are promised when one celebrates it. Everybody should always perform the worship of *Devī* in order to secure incomparable eminence which confers the aims of life viz. *Dharma, Artha, Kāma,* and *Mokṣa,* and one should worship her for the happiness in life,[141] for the destrucsion of evil spirits and for delight. The original purpose and objects of this festival were high and noble as stated in *Devī purāṇa,*. "This is a great *Vrata* conferring benefits on all the people, and vanquishing all their enemies. It should be performed by the *Brāhmins* for solemn sacrifices, and by the *Kshatriyas* for the protection of the people, by the *Vaiśyas* for cattle wealth, by the *Śudras* with desire of sons and happiness. By women for blessed wifehood and by the rich people for more wealth.[142] *Devī Mahātmya* attaches great importance to it saying that by performing this Vrata a man becomes free from all troubles and is endowed with wealth and crops.[143] The *Bhaviṣya Purāṇa*[144] goes to the extent that all the sacrifices described in the *Vedas* and the *Śāstras* are not equal even to one hundredth part of this worship. But in the later periods, the objects were brought down to the ordinary level or below level and this *Vrata* was performed for the black actions in the medieval ages.

Adhikāris

This worship is very much cosmopolitan in character and it could be performed not only by *Dvijas* but even by those who were outside the pale of the caste system.[145] All this occassion the worship has a social element also in it (such as inviting friends and feeding them), the goddess *Durgā* is worshipped by the various groups of *Mlechhas,* by the *Dasyus,* by the people from *Anga, Banga and Kalinga* countries and by the *Kinnaras, Barbaras and Sakas.*[146] Only one condition was there, that the devotees should be full of devotion, should have taken bath and should be cheerful and jolly.[147]

The worship of *Durgā* is of three fold character, viz. *Sātviki* worship, consisting of *Japa* and offering of vegetarian *Naivaidya, Rājasi* worship, is effected by *Bali, and offering of Naiviedya* containing meat, and *Tāmasi* worship is effected by the offerings of wine, and meat, etc. The tāmasi worship is performed even without *Mantras* (prevalent among the *Kirātas*).[148]

PUJĀ

It is known to every Hindu that the deities are deemed to go to sleep for four months from *Āsādha to Kārtika.* As *Durgā* is also asleep *in Āsvina*, therefore the first step in the worship is rousing of *Devī* (*Bodhana*) from sleep.[149] The devotee, begins on the first *Tithi* of *Āsvina* bright half and the *bodhana* takes place on the 6th of the bright half. On the first *tithi* he places, *Ghaṭa,* full of water and mango-leaves and then worships *Durgā* with 16 *Upacāras.*[150] On the Second day he offers a silken ribbon for keeping the hair in position. On the third day *Alaktaka* dye for reddening the feet, and a mirror is offered. On the fourth *tithi* *Madhūparka* is offered to the goddess, while on the fifth day he offers sandal wod paste, unguents, and ornaments according to his means. The *Kālika Purāṇa* summarises the acts tobe performed from the fourth *tithi* to the ninth respectively.[151]

The principal items in the *Navrātra* worship or *Durgāpūjā,* thought it may be spread over three dayes (from 7th), or nine days, (from 1st to 9th) are four as laid down by the

Linga Purāṇa viz. *Snāpana* (bathing the image), *Pūjā* the offering of *Bāli* and performance of *Homa.*[152] Though the bathing is said to be one of the most important item but in the Purāṇas it is substituted by the *Bodhna* ceremony, all and these are described in detail as follows—

Bodhana

On the 6th day, he should go in the morning near a *bilva* tree and utter a *Sankalpa,* establish a *Ghaṭa* and worship the *Bilva* tree as *Durgā,* and in the evening he should rouse Devi with the recitation of the Mantras.[153] After the awakening of Devi, she sould be placed on a *bilva* tree, making a dwelling place for her, along with the materials viz. clay, sandalwood paste, *durvā,* grass, flowers, *rochanā,* gold, silver, mirror, lamp etc., and then he should come to the *panḍal* erected for *Durgā-pūjā.*[154]

Worship

The devotee should offer worship to the nine plants[155] and to the image of *Durgā* and make the *Devī* abide in the *bilva* tree. Then in the 7th morning he should offer the *bali* of boiled rice, for protection against the evil spirits. He should worship the goddess with salutations and with *Upacaras,* perform the *Praṇa-Pratiṣṭha* ceremony and contemplate upon the form of Devī. He should put a flower on his head and make an invocation (*Avāhana*) with *mantras* to *Durgā* to be present in the *bilva branch* and establish her with the prayer to bestow longlife, health and prosperity. The worship of Devī in the *Ghaṭa* along with flowers takes place with separate *Mantras.* Then he should worship *Durgā* with *Pādya* and other *Upacāras,*[156] with due regards *Ārati* takes place and last of all *Dakshinā* is offered. The sixteen *Upacāras,* used in the worship of *Durgā* are slightly different, from the usual *Upachāras* in the worship of other gods.[157] The *Kālikā Purāṇa* contains a long dissertation on the 16 *Upacāras* and Special discussions are about the fragrent substances, flowers, *Naivaidya,* wine, fruits, etc. to be used in the goddess worship.[158] The worship is performed on 8th and 9th of bright *Āsvin,* but on the 9th day it is simply repetition of the process of the worship performed on 8th.

Having worshipped the goddess, he should offer a kind on the night of eighth, and on the 9th *tithi* also. The kid or he buffallow should be dark in complexion and at least five years old.[159] The *Kālikā purāṇa* gives a long list of the nanes of the animals to be offered to the goddess.[160] It includes in the list even the name of human being as well as the blood of one's own self. But it bans the females, and young ones of any one of the mentioned.[161] still only the goats ad he-buffaloes were sacrificed.[162] The *Kālikā Purāṇa* is bold enough to attach great importance to the offering of human being, by giving the name of *Bali, Mahābali* and *Atibali* for goats, he-buffaloes and human beings respectively.[163] It has to be remembered that though an animal is killed still what is offered to *Devī* is generally blood and the head of the victim.[164] This purified blood and head of the victim offered to Devi was called *Pīyusha,* meaning nector.

The *Kālikā Purāṇa* and the *Tantras* prescribe an elaborate ritual about the killing of the *bali Paśu* and offering its blood and head to the goddess.[165] The rites and the *Mantras* differ slightly according to the *bali* of a goat, he-buffaloe, or the devotee's own blood. The *bali* animal is made to face east, while the *sādhaka* faces the north and repeats the *Mantras.*[166] He should place the flowers on the head of the victim, sprinkle water and worships the sword with the *Mantra.* "You are the tongue of *Chanḍikā* and you accomplish heaven for the worshipper." Then he worships the victims and with one stroke cuts off the head of the victim. He collects the blood in a vessel, places it before Devi, and offers it to the goddess with *Mantras.* He offers the head of the victim and makes a *Tilaka* on his forehead with the blood of the victim. Then he performs *Japa* of the certain *Mantra* and also some verses of laudation and asks for certain benefits.[167] Though vegetarian substitutes for *Bali* to *Devī*[168] are also prescribed, and some families of higher castes as well as sectaries of vaishnavism practise it.[169] but the goats and buffaloes are offered to *Devī* by saying that a victim offered in a sacrffice to *Devī* goes to heaven and those who till him incur no sin.[170]

On *Mahāṣṭamī* day a devotee has to observe a fast, keep himself pure and observe the rules for *Vrata,*[171] and worship *Devī*. On this very day he has to honour maidens, feed them and *Brahmins*. Though daily worship of the maidens is prescribed but he must do so at least on *mahaṣṭamì* day. *Devī Purāṇa* attaches the highest merit to the honouring of maidens i.e.[172] the Girls, varying in age from two to ten years, are honoured with bodice, clothes, flowers, edibles and so on. *Devī Purāṇa* also prescribes the worship of the married ladies.[173]

Recitation of *Devī Mahātmya* or listening to it is said to be of great importance for all the nine days[174] The offerings of seasum, curds, milk, ghee, meat etc. are casted into the fire by reciting the *Mantras.*[175] The *Mantras* are called *Jayanti Mantras,* and the offerings may be poured by reciting the verses of *Devī Māhātmya* of *Mārkanḍeva Purāṇa.*[176] Last of all the *Nirāgana* is performed.[177]

After every *Pujā* prescribed for the day, the family members, their friends and guests sit together and partake of *Praśāda.* They also participate in music, dance or *Kīrtana* while awakening in the night.[178] In this way this festival is celebrated in honour of *Durga* with great enthusiasm, and with full paraphernalia.

On the 10th *tithi* after bathing and sipping water, the devotee should offer worship with 16 *upacāras,* should praise *Devī* with the words "*Om Durgāṃ Śivaṁ,*" should prostrate before her and make a request to Devi with the *Mantra*

"*Mahiṣāghni Mahāmāye* and with other verses,[179] take a flower and cast it on the image with the words forgive. Then he should raise the image of Devi, the bilva twig and nine plants and place them at another place, also lamps before them. The devotees should to go a river while performing dance, song, music, auspicious recitations and sports and immerse the image in the water after making a prayer[180] Then performance of *Śabarotsavam* the *Kālikā Purāṇa* dwells on this at great length saying 'that immersion of Devi's image should be made in the festivals in the manners of *Śabaras* i.e. people may make merry to their hearts content by indulging in sports and festivities.[181] This provision that every one, high or low, has to join the *Śabarotsava*—probably emphasized that before *Devī* everyone is of equal status and should perform this function on the 10th day to show the equality of humanity at large.[182]

Paśubali or Bali

Animal sacrifice is an established rite celebrated for the goddess. Even the *Purāṇic* literature abounds in instances and prescribes *Paśubali*;[183] though it follows the *Dakshināchārī* system of worship. Generally this *Paśubali* was offered to the goddess *Candikā* on *Navami tithi,* especially in *Navarātra* days. The *Devī Bhāgāvata Purāṇa* says that this is not *Himsā* and it justifies the killing of the animals if they are offered to the goddess by saying that they will go to heaven and no sin will be incurred on the killer.[184] But the *Purāṇa* says that it is meant only for those, who are habituated to take meat etc.[185] The *Kālikā Purāṇa* also makes a prohibition of *Paśubali* by the *Brāhmanas.*[186] It is only the *Kālikā Purāṇa* which deals in detail with the process of *Paśubali.* This has been dealt within *Navarātra* ceremony.

Devī Purāṇa says that only those animals who are five years old, and perfectly in good health should be offered to the goddess, in the midnight of *Mahāṣṭāmī or Mahānavamī*[187]

Still we find that this *Bali* was offered generally to the *Ugra* forms of *Devī* and not to the *Saumya* forms or *Sātvikī* godesses. We find a list of animals to be offered. This list of sacrificial animals enumerated in the *Kālikā Purāṇa*[188] is very wide: viz. birds, tortoises, alligators, fish, nine species of wild animals, buffaloes, bulls, he-goats, wild boars rhinoceros, antelopes, iguanas, rein-deer, lions, and tigers.[189] Blood drawn from one's own body may also be offered.[190] Ordinarily females of all the animals are exempted from seacrifice,[191] but when mass sacrifices are offered, the distinction between the male and female is not observed. The horses and the elephants are not accepted by the goddess, they are meant only for special sacrifices by the Kings.[192] The *Yogini Tantra* enlarges the list and includes also monkey amongst sacrificial animals. While worshipping the goddess on the cremation ground only the buffaloes sacrificed,[193] and spirituous liquor is a constant accompaniment to the blood offering.[194]

This list seems to be made up of the various animals sacrificed by different tribal groups. Amongst the Singphos, Lushais and the Garos, dogs are sacrificed on various occasions, amongst the Garos dogs are sacrificed only at the time of cremation, the idea being that the spirit of the deceased would lose its way.[195] Now dogs came also into reference in the menu of Hindu offerings to. In a place called *Aśva Tirtha* offerings to the spirit of the dead could be made. The offerings might consist of pure vegetables or flesh. The flesh of all the animals could be offered excepting that of bulls and dogs, which was prohibited in the Kali era.[196]

Though this rite is very ancient prevailing in the pre-Āryan stages—still it enjoys very important place in the *Tantras,* and the *Purāṇas* also mention it but with a hesitation. From time to time the *Purāṇas* go on saying that this is *Tāmasī* worship and this worship is meant for the kings only and this should not be by everyone.[197] All this goes to show that the *Purāṇas* were assimilating the practices of the *Tantras* but with some precautions and modifications.

Human sacrifice

The Human sacrifice or offering of human flesh, find mention in the *Ṛigveda*[198] and other *Vedic* literature, at time of performing the *Aśvamedha* sacrifice.[199] The man who is to be slaughtered must be neither a priest nor a slave, but a warrior or a man of the third caste (*Kshatriya or Vaiśya*). This practice find place also in *Śaktism,* and the *Śākta Purāṇas* abound in the various instances or exhortations regarding this practice of human sacrifice.[200]

The *Kālikā Purāṇa* gives very interesting details regarding the performance of the human sacrifice.[201] Having placed the victim before the goddess, the worshipper should adore her by offering flowers, sandal paste and bark, frequently repeating the *Mantra,* appropriate for sacrifice.[202] Then, facing the North and placing the victim to face the East, he should look backward and repeat this Mnatra: "O man, through my good fortune thou hast appeard as a victim; therefore, I have thee; thou uniform and of the form of a victim. Thou by gratifying *Cāndikā,* destroyest all evil incidents to the giver. Thou, a victim who appearest as a sacrifice meat, for the *Vaiṣṇavī,* hast my saluations. The Victims were created by the self-born himself for sacrificical rites; I shall slaughter thee to-day, and slaughter as a sacrifice is no murder." Thus meditating on that human-formed victim, a flower should be thrown on the top of his head with the Mantra[203]: "O sword, thou art the tongue of *Candikā* and bestower of the region of the gods. Black and holding the trident, thou art like the last dreadful night of creation; born fierce, of bloody eyes and mouth, wearing a blood-red garland, salutations be to thee." The sword, having thus been consecrated, should be taken up while repeating the *Mantra*: "*Oṁ, huṁ phat*" and the excellent victim be slautered with it. There ofted, carefully sprinkling the blood of the victim, water, rock-salt, honey, aromatics, and flowers, it should be placed before the goddess, and the skull also, with a lamp burning over it, should be placed before her with the *Mantra*: "*Oṁ Aiṁ, Hriṁ, Śriṁ, Kauśiki,* thou art may be gratified with the blood."[204]

It is again stated in connection with the sacrifice of animals and human beings: men,[205] and blood drawn from the offerers own body, are looked upon as proper oblations to the goddess *Candikā.*[206] By a human sacrifice, *Devī* is pleased for 1000 years, and by the sacrifice of three people for 100,000 years.[207]

Bāṇa, the famous Sanskrit poet refers to the sale of human flesh.[208] The *Mālati-Mādhava* of *Bhavabhūti* relates how *Mādhava*, the hero, tries to win the favour of the ghouls of the cemetery by the offering of human flesh, and comes to a temple of *Cāmundā* just in time to save his beloved *Mālati,* from being sacrificed to the Goddess by *Aghoraghantā,* the priest, and his associate *Kapālakundalā.*[209] This is a singular instance wherein a female is meant to be sacrificed. The *Kathāsaritasāgara* of *Somadeva* gives many instances of human sacrifice in honour of *Candikā* or *Cāmundā.* 'One Muravara, a Turushka or Indo-Scythina, proposed to make a human sacrifice in the memory of his dead father. An expiatory sacrifice to the *Candikā* to save the life of a king is mentioned.[210]

Offering of one's own head or blood to the Goddess:

Offering of his own blood to a deity for the acquisition of religious merit in the next world had been an established institution in our country from early times.[211] It is, specially in the ritual works of the *Śākṭa* sect that we have clear directions for the devotee's offer of his own flesh and blood to the great goddess.[212] In the *Mārkanḍeya Purāṇa* we are told how King *Suratha* and a merchant *Samadhi*—

erected her image and propitiated her with various offerings including those soaked with blood from their own bodies.[213] The goddess being thus propitiated appeared before them and granted them all their desires.[214]

How the goddess becomes satisfied for one thousand years, by the offering of one's own blood and how she fulfils all desires in six months' time when one offers her a small piece of flesh close to his heart, is told in the *Kālikā Purāṇa.*[215] The *Kumāri Tantra* quoted in the *Tantrasāra* promises boon of royalty to one, who offers blood from his own body.[216] The *Matsya Sūkta* of the *Mahā Tantra* quoted in the Prāṇa *Toṣiṇi* compares the merits of different kinds of blood-offerings including that of his own body, by the devotee to the goddess.[217]

It is a matter of common knowledge that the rite of offering the blood, nearest the heart before the Goddess is much observed by pious Hindu ladies of our country, down in our own tiems.[218] It is interesting to note here that the ritual works of *Śākta* sect seek to impose a ban upon the observance of this rite by the *Brahmins.* The texts *viz. Kālikā Purāṇa—Tantrasāra*; *Gāyatri Tantra* quoted in *Hara Tattva Didhiti,* forbid a *Brāhmine* to offer blood from his own body to the goddess.[219]

In the secular Sanskrit literature we find the mention of the rite. We may refer to a number of stories belonging to *Vikramāditya,* the king, who in favour of some suffering mortal, prepares to strike at his own neck with his sword, and thus propitiates the goddess, for granting him the necessary favour.[220] There is also a story of *Rājputra Viravara* who is said to have actually cut off his own head as an offering to the goddess *Candikā* for the purpose of saving his royal master from his impending doom.[221]

We may draw out some conclusion from this that the rite of head-offering was performed mostly for the propitiation of the Goddess *Durgā* to win some favour for the devotee himself or for others, and in some cases purely in a spirit of supreme sacrifice.

Devotion—the means of realisation

The aim of all higher forms of religion seems to be the realisation of the ultimate reality. The followers of the *Bhakti* school regard devotion—(*bhakti*) as the essential and the most effective means to the realisation of the Absolute, unless *Jñāna, yoga* and *karma* are not attended with devotion, they are incapable of producing their respective results and work entirely in vain.[222] The *Bhaktimārga* lays special stress on the personality of God and regards the Personal God as the Absolute or the Highest Reality. Like all theistic religions, it emphasises the duality involved in the relationship.[223] The distinction between the finite personality and the Absolute, seems to be essential to the concept of *Bhakti*. In this respect it differs considerably from other paths. *Sādhanā* in *Bhakti mārga* seems to be comparatively easier to most of the persons. It is easy because it follows the objective path and deals with concrete things. It places before the devotee an object that attracts and interests his mind—and by this attraction the individual and the Absolute are linked together. Here it is said that one should enjoy in order to realise the truth underlying the object of enjoyment and should not be so much engrossed with the object as to be deprived of the capacity of looking beyond it to its source.[224]

All the *Purāṇas* dealing with *Śakti* worship preach the path of devotion, as the only means to realise the Absolute *Parā Śakti*. *Devī Bhāgavata Purāṇa* which is considered a compendium of devotion to the goddess, gives extra importance to *Bhakt Yoga*. Generally the devotion towards goddess is *Mātṛ-Bhakti*,[225] unlike the Vaiṣṇavism where the *Bhakti* is either in the form of *Dāsya Bhāva or Sakhya Bhāva*—which means that either the devotee establishes his relation with the god as Master and servant or as a friend.

She is Mother of all and complete surrender to the goddess is prescribed.[226] *Śakti*, like God *Kṛṣṇa* in the *Gīta*, in *Devī Bhāgavata*, speaks to her devotees, saying that whoever surrenders to me is always dear to me.[227] The *Mārkanḍya Purāṇa* says that when worshipped with devotion, the goddess gives *Bhukti* and *Mukti* both.[228] There are *Devī Gitās* in *Devī Bhāgavata Purāṇa, Devī Purāṇa* and *Mahābhāgavata Purāṇa* dealing with the topic of devotion to the goddess. In *Devī Bhāgavata Bhakti* is called of three types viz. *Sātvikī, Rājasī,* and *Tāmasī* and last of all *Turiyā Bhakti* or *Parā Bhakti* is also mentioned which is identified with knowledge or *Vairagya.*[229] Devi says that whoever is devoted to me becomes invincible,[230] even the gods headed by *Indra, Viṣṇu, Śiva* and others will not be able to do any harm to the devotees of *Śakti*. The devotion of Devi consists mainly of three things *viz.* recitation of *Japa* of the names, (*Nāmajapa*), worship with *Śraddhā* and praising of the goodess (*Stavana*).[231] The *Śākta Purāṇas* generally say that one should be devoted to Her lotus feet. In *Devī Bhāgavata* we find mention of *Navadhā Bhatī.*[232]

The *Kālikā Purāṇa* goes to the extant that one should rememebr Her while taking food, going for a journey, and while attending some social or cultural function.[233] A *Śākta* has to identify himself in meditaiton with the *Śakti,*[234] he worships and places before himself the fully blossomed condition represented but the diety as the ideal to be realised. Here the *Purāṇas* follow the *Tantric* motto that "देवो भूत्वा `दव यजेत" The *Śākta Purāṇas* on this point differ from the usual*Bhakti Marga,* where dualism is an established step. We find the complete identification of the devotee with the deity, a stage higher than the complete merger or surrender to the deity, preached by the *Bhāgavatas.*[235]

Devotees of Śakti in the Purāṇas

The *Purāṇas* have given some details with regard to the worshippers of *Śakti.* The *Mārkaṇḍeya Purāṇa* contains a description of *Śakti* worship as celebrated by *Suratha* and *Samādhi.* They worshipped an earthen image of *Durgā* with all solemnity on the bank of the river. Their adoraiton, intense and selfless, was rewarded with success and the great Mother appeared beofre them to grant their passionate prayer.[236]

According to the current tradition and the *Sākta Purāṇas* *Rāma* was the first to celebrate the worship of the Great Mother (*Durgā*) on the eve of the great war that ensued between himself and *Rāvaṇa.* It is stated in the *Purāṇas* that *Rāma* untimely awakened the Goddess, since he was in a hurry to bring about the ruin of his formidable rival. The worship of *Śakti* is calculated to have given him so much strength that he could easily come out victorious from the terrible warfare. This celebration took place in the month of *Aśvina,* and since then the autumn is regarded as specially sacred occassion for the invocation and adoraiton of the Goddess.[237] The *Bhāgavata Purāṇa* narrates the worship of the goddess *Kātyāyanī* by the damsels of *Vraja* by the *Yadàvas,*[238] and by *Rukmini.*

Viṣṇu is said to have performed a sacrifice (*Ambikāyājña*) according to the āganika rites the sake of recuring the good grace of the Divine Mother.[239] He was a devout fllower of *Śakti.* The king Sudarśana, son of Dhruvasandhi, was a descendant of the solar dynasty. In his early life he had to fight against many odds and was in a state of utter destitution. While a mere boy, he was, however, initiated into *kāmabīja* in a mysterious way and Constant repetition of the sacred syllable conferred all the blessings upon him.[240] Having regained the lost kingdom of his father, *Sudarśana* went to *Ayodhyā* and built a beautiful temple there and placed the image of he Great Mother in a right royal fashion and Since that time the worship of the Goddess has been prevalent in *Kośala*[241] *Subāhu,* the king of *Kāśi,* simiarly made a temple at Benaras and establihed the image of *Durgā* which is still visited by the innumerable pilgrims.[242]

The wife of *Jayatsena,* was king of *Kāshi* a worshipper of *Gauri.*[243] The king *Śūdraka* was a devotee of *Devī* [244] and similarly the King *Devapanna* is said to have been a worshipper of *Camundā.*[245] The King *Nahuṣa* is also described to have worshipped the goddess on the seventh day of the bright half of the month of *Bhādrapada.*[246] The kings *Aja* and *Raghu* also worshipped *Bhairavī.*[247] The king *Mahānandi* worhsipped *Mahālakṣmī* at *Magadha.*[248] The King *Naraka* was a keen devotee of *Kāmākhya.*[249] The King *Rupasena of Vardhananagara* and his wife offered thier son as a Bali in a sacrifice: but he was revived again.[250] *Patañjali* is said to have defeated *Kali* with the help of the blessings of the Goddess."[251] Further the followings are described as being the worshippers of the Mother-Goddess; King *Satyavrata* of the *Ikṣvāku* dynasty,[252] *Yājnavalkya,*[253] *Dharmadhvaja,*[254] *Sumada* (worshipper of *Kāmāksī*), [255] *Kārttavirya*, who possessed the *Kavaca of Bhadrakālī,* and others.[256]

Devī Purāṇa mentions so many devoteess of *Devīs*, specially they are either kings or the rulers of states. A king of Kanchi is said to be the *Bhakta* of *Devī,* he was fond of wine and meat and was enemical towards the *Bràhmins,* the gods and the teacher.[257] The *Puràṇa* says that *Paraśurāma* worshipped *Durgā* and constructed a temple of *Durgā* at *Ayodhyā.* According to the *Kālikā Purāṇa VaŸiŸâha* and *Naraka* were devout devotees of *Śakti,* even the *Prajāpati Daksh* and *Himvān* are said to be the *Bhaktas* of *Devī.*[258] The *Māhābhāgavata Purāṇa* says that the *Pāṇḍavas* were devout followers of *Śakti.*[259] According to this *Purāṇa* even *Rāvāna* was her devotee. *Devī Bhāgavata* says that all the forteen Manus were her devotees.[260] The *Purāṇa* also mentions the name of *Prahlāda,*[261] *Indrāṇī,*[262] *Hariścandra,*[263] *Yuvanaśva,*[264] *Nara-Nārāyana,*[265] *Śukadeva,*[266] *Madhu-*

Kaitabha,[267] *Śiva,*[268] *Brahmā,*[269] *Vyāsa,*[270] *Kûṣṇa,*[271] *Agastya*[272] and others as the devotees of *Devī.*[273] Thus we see that *Śaktism* had become a popular cult by the time of the *Purāṇas,* and *Śakti* was given a highly elevated position in the *Hindu* pantheon.

Devī Vratas

There is a large number of *Vratas* mentioned in *the* Purāṇas and the *Upa-purāṇas,* pertaining to *Devī.* The *Purāṇas* have also given a code of conduct to be observed by the devotees of Devi.

Fast

Observing a fast is the essential step of these rules, and on the preceding day of the *Vrata* one has to practise abstinence and restraint both in one's food and personal habits. On the proper day he has to observe fast and then, on the following day he has to take a very simple diet, avoiding wine, meat etc.

Donations

Besides the observance of a fast the most important item is the honouring and feeding of the *Brāhmaṇas* and girls and liberally making gifts to them.[274] Among the items of the gifts, gold, land, and cow rank the highest. Among other things are included, metals, pots, daily necessaries of life, like sugar, paddy, cloths, blankets, fan, footwear as well as all other articles of worship.

Results

The majority of the *Vratas* are supposed to produce tangible results. Their performer is endowed with a beautiful form, and he gets immense fortune, subdues the enemy, and is rendered free from all earthly calamities including vairous diseases. The issueless person gets a son, the poor becomes a rich, wife can ensure the welfare and love of the husband, one can regain his lost kingdom or property, and one separated from one's near and dear relations can be re-united with them. In short, all conceivable temporal bliss can be attained. The attainment of both the *Bhukti* and *Mukti* associated with the performance of these *Vratas*.

Ladies

Though both, men and women are entitled to perfrom these *Vratas,* yet these seem to be primarily intended for laides—married or un-married or widowed. By performing these *Vratas* and worshipping the benign form of the goddess, the ladies gain the freedom of their husbands and sons from all maladies, happiness and long life and ensure the love of their husbands. Thus in a way these *Vratas* seem to have been a means of keeping the woman folk within the fold of family life by giving the various assurances of a happy existence here and hereafter.[275]

In these *Vratas generally the Devī*'s clay-idol was obtained and was worshipped with vegetarian *Naivaidya* by the ladies, to procure either health of their children, a good husband, *Saubhāgya,* prosperity, happiness, and removal of the fear from all sorts of danger. These *Vratas* are full of festivities, followed with, dancing, music and marry-making by the children and ladies.[276] Thus the cult of *Śakti* was consisting of *Vratas* which is the characteristic of *Paurāṇika* religion.

Days:—For *Durgā* or Mothers, *Navamī* is said the proper *Tithi* for worship, दुर्गायै नवमी मता'[277] and *Caṇḍikā* or *Caṇḍī* is also worshipped on *Navamī*[278] *while Gauri* and *Umā* are to be worshipped on *Tṛtīyā.*[279] The night of *Āśvina-Śukla-Aṣṭamī* is considered the very auspicious day for *Devi Pūjā* by the authors of the *Purāṇas.*[280] In this way the *Devī Vratas* are generally observed either on *Tṛtīyā or Navamī* days and especially of the bright fortnight.

VṚATAS PERFORMED ON TṚTĪYA

1. ***Madhūka Tṛtīyā Vratam or Gaurī Vratam***: (third date of *Phālguna*): This Vrata is observed by the ladies specially unmarried girls to obtain a good husband.[281] *Gaurī* sitting in a chariot yoked by Godha-bull, is to be worshipped with *Gandha, Dhūpa*, sandal, sweat meats, and golden ornaments. Then the *Brāhmanas* and the girls be fed & singing as well as dancing programmes should be arranged.

This is also performed on the third day of the month of *Vaiśākha*, *Bhādrapvda* and *Māgha* and is called *Saubhāgya Karana Vrata*,[282] Salt is forbidden duing the Vrata and the donation of a bed with bedsheets etc. is praised verymuch.[283] This worship of the goddess in a *Madhuka* tree is also prescribed by *Devī Bhāgavata Purāṇa*[284] on *Chaitra Śukla Tṛītyā*.

2. ***Gaurī Tṛitīyā Vratam***: According to the *Padma Purāṇa* and the *Bhaviṣya Purāṇa*[285] it is observed on the third day of *Śrāvana, Vaiśākha* and *Mārgaśiras,*' in respect of *Garuī*,[286] and is called *Gaurivratam* or *Saubhāgya vratam*. While according to the *Nārada Purāṇa* it should be celebrated continuosly for 12 months, starting from *Chaitra*, and the *Purāṇa* gives 12 different names of *Garuī*[287] The *Brahma Vaivarta Purāṇa* says that it is performed on *Mārgasrsa Sankrānti* day.[288] Bathing of *Devī* with milk, honey, scented water and offering of the fruits and flower—is prescribed. Pūjā is performed and the *Kamala* flower having 16 leaves is to be inscribed.[289] Then feeding of the ladies and offering to them the silken clothes, gives the devotee health, prosperity, and sinless life etc. In the end of *Vrata* the beddings to the couples numbering 24 or 12 or eight or four—are offered. Guru is to be respected first of all and then others.[290] Flowers to be offered in the different months are: red flowers, blue lotuses, *Bandhujīva, Jāti flower*, yellow flowers, Kunda, *Sindhuvāra, Aśoka, GandhaPāṭala,*

lotus, *Jalāmbuja, Mandar or Mālati* etc. starting from *Bhādrapada* to *Śrāvaṇa* respectively.[291] This Vrata is observed for 12 years by the ladies or girls. The accounts given in the *Padma* and *Matsya Purāṇas* are very much similar.[292]

3. ***Umā Vratam***—also called *Guḍa Vrata* (*Tṛtīyā of Caitra* and *Māgha*). It is to be performed by every body with all the paraphernalia of the worship, to gain happiness in the life.[293] The *Padma Purāṇa* says that in this *Vrata, Guḍa* in a large quantity should be offered.[294] The *Vrata* is also called *Mahāvratam* and The *Brahma Vaivarta Purāṇa* calls it as *Jai Durgā Vratam*—because the *Gopīs* worshipped in the month of *Māgha*, the goddess, called—*Jaya Durgā*.[295]

4. ***Umā Maheśvara Vratam***: 1. It is observed by the ladies to obtain progeny, health love of their husband,and prosperity in the life.[296] It is Celeberated on *Mārga Śirsaśukla-Tṛtīyā*, the goddess *Lalitā* and *Śiva* both[297] are worshipped and *Dhūpa, Dipaka* sandal and *Naivaidya* should be offered to both. Having observed it for 12 months, one should give the images of *Śiva* and *Umā* to the *Brāhmins*.

2. *This vrata* is mentioned in the *Skanda Purāṇa* also.[298] It is performed on *Aṣṭamī* or *Caturthī* of *Caitra* and *Mārga Śīrṣa*. It is said here that *Śiva* and *Pārvatī* are to be offered *Pūjā* according to *Āgama Vidhān*.[299]

5. ***Raṁbha Vratam or Rambha Tṛtīyā Vratam:*** It is celebrated continuously for full one year, on various *Tṛtīyās* of *Śukla Pakṣa* starting from *Mārga-śīrsa*. The names of the goddesses of different months are: *Pārvatī, Sudevī, Gaurī, Viśālākṣi, Śrīmukhi, Mādhavī, Śrī; Hara Tālī,Giriputrī, Padmodbhavā,* etc. only ten names are there. The worship is performed in the night with full paraphernalia of the *Pūjā-vidhāna*,[300] on *Āśvina Śukla-Tṛtīyā* it is celebrated with much festivity by the ladies for their *Saubhāgya* and beauty as well as to overpower their co-wives. *Devī* is offered all the *Upacāras*, then *Havan* takes place and people become happy in life[301] *Donations* may be given to a married *Brāhmaṇa*

and they should be fed on *Caturthī*.

6. ***Ārdrānandakarī Tṛītyā Vratam*:** It is observed on any *Śukla Tṛtīyā* when *Āṣaḍha* constellation takes place. The goddess *Bhavānī* is worshipped by the ladies and different kinds of flowers, specially of white colour are offered to *Śiva* and *Bhavānī*. The Devotees get *Saubhāgya*, pleasure, and prosperity.[302]

There is mention of the names of *Devī*s in the *Mantras* to be recited during worship. These are[303]: *Vāsudevī, Śokavināśinī, Raôbha, Āditi, Mādhavī, Ānandakarī, Utkandhini, Indrāṇi*, and *Viśvamukhī*. It is also described in the *Matsya Purāṇa* and the similarity between the two accounts goes to show that one has been borrowed from antoher.[304] It is mentioned also as one of the important *Vrata* of *Devī* in the *Padma Purāṇa*.[305] Here it is said that by the performance of this *Vrata* a man may get even *Ātamānaœda*.[306] Beddings and cots are also offered to the Brahmins for the pleausre of *Devī*.[307]

7. ***Rasa-Kalyāṇinī Vratam*:** It is Observed either on *Bhādrapada Śukla* or *Vaiśākha Śukla Tûtīyā*. or *Marga Śirśa Śukla Tûtīyā*. The Goddess *Lalitā* is to be worshipped with milk and honey, *Tilā* and rice, and white flowers and fruits. *Gita-mangala Dhavani* is to be made. In the end feeding of the *Brahmins* and girls, donations of gold, and bedding and worship of Guru—all these are prescribed. Devotee gets his all his desires fulfilled.[308]

According to the *Matsya Purāṇa* it is celebrated for full one year starting from *Mīgha Śukla Tûâīya*[309] and *Devī* is to be bathed with water, mixed with *Tila*, and honey. In this *Vrata* devotee has to abondon the use of salt in his food. After the completion of one year in the *Māgha* month—an image of *Devī* made of gold and two cows should be denoted for the pleasure of the goddess.[310]

One has to abandon the following articles in different

months, salt, sugar, oil, honey, water, *Jirakam,*milk, curd, Ghee, honey, food grains, and sugar starting from *Māgha* to *Mārgaśiras.*[311] So many names of the goddess are mentioned to be recited,[312] *viz. Lalitā, Śāntā, Śrī, Kamalā, Rudrāṇī, Śankarā, Viśvavasinī, Kānti, Mohanā, Amṛtā, Gaurī, Bhavānī,* and *Kāmadevī.*

8. *Harakāli Tṛtīyā Vratam:* The goddess *Harakāli,* beloved of *Śiva* is to be praised on *Bhādra Pada Śukla Tṛtīya,* called as *Harakāli Tṛtiyā.* With full details of the worship and the constituents, mainly vegetarian and with full festivity including dance ad music—she is to be worshipped. In the night, the *Jāgaraṇa* and the recitation of the *Kāthā* should be arranged. Next morning *Devī* is to be immersed in the water witht the recitation of Mantras and Then feeding of the *Brahmins* and the girls takes place.[313]

9. *Saubhāgyaśṭaka Tṛtīyā Vratam:* The *Vrata* is observed for full one year starting from the *Tṛtīyā* of *Vasant Māsa* (*Caitra*). This is celebrated on the *Tṛtīyā* of every month and the goddesss *Gaurī* or *Lalitā* is to be worshipped with her husband *Śiva*—and the idols of both be given to the *Brahmins* after completing the *Vrata* for one year. The beddings and other luxuries of the life may be donated. In this way it can be observed for 12 years or 8 or seven years and the devotee gets wealth, health, happiness, good partner in life and the final salvation.[314] Names of the 12 goddesses presiding over different months,[315] are mentioned here. This very *Vrata* in *Agni Purāṇa,* is called *Mūla-Gaurī Vrata,* having all the *Vidhāna* as prescribed in the *Bhaviṣya Purāṇa*[316] and *Padma Purāṇa* also calls it *Saubhāgya* sayana Vratam and the eight articles are to be donated.[317]

10. *Lalitā Tṛitīyā Vratam:* It is observed in every month for one year starting from *Māgha Śukla.* Ladies clad in silk, worship the goddess with *Bilvas, Āmalaka,* scented flowers and *Dhūpa, Dīpaka,* and *Naivaidya.* Donation is prescribed and night sleep is banned on that day. ext day also *Devī* is worshipped with all the upacharas.[318]

11. *Aviyoga Tṛitīyā Vratam:* To obtain *Sukha* and good luck, ladies both married or widows observed it on *Mrāga-Śiras-Śukla-Tṛtiyā.* It is also performed for one year and *Gaurī,* and *Śiva* both are worshipped. Performance of *Havana,* feeding of the *Brāhmanas* and the masses, and *Pujā* are the main items of this *Vrata.* Starting from *Kārtiḳa* it comes to an end in the month of *Mārghaśiras.*[319]

Names of the goddesses and gods to be worshipped.[320]

1. *Gaurī—Śiva—Mārgaśiras*
2. *Pārvati—Giriśa—Pausha*
3. *Bhavānī—Bhava—Māgha*
4. *Umā—Mahādeva—Phālguna*
5. *Lalitā—Śankara—Caitra*
6. *Lolanetrā—Sthāṇu—Vaiśākha*
7. *Ekvirā—Vireśvara—Jyeṣṭha*
8. *Śakṭi—Paśupatinatha—Āṣāḍha*
9. *Sutā—Śrī Kaṇṭha—Śrāvaṇa*
10. *Durgā—Bhima—Bhādrapada*
11. *Durgā—Śiva—Āśvina*
12. *Śivā—Issāna—Kārtika*

12. *Anantara Tṛtiya Vratam:* It is observed on all the *Tṛtiyas of Kṛṣṇa Pakṣa* and *Śukla Pakṣa* of every month. Though it is said that it benefits everybody still for, the ladies it is more helpful,[321] and for different months different things are prescribed for *Naivaidya.*

1. *Mārgaśiras*—coconut
2. *Pauṣa*—Sweat meats
3. *Māgha—Bilva*
4. *Phālgun—Puris*
5. *Chaiṭra—Pīṣṭa*
6. *Vaiśākha—Srī khaṇḍa*
7. *Jyeṣṭha—Mangoes*
8. *Āṣādha—Sattu*
9. *Śrāvana—Godhūma*
10. *Bhādrapada—Kulmāṣa*
11. *Āśvina—Khandapupa*

12. *Kārtika—Khira*

Performance of *Havana,* fast, worship, recitation of *Nāma,* giving of alms, offering of clothes, ornaments, and even cosmetics, *Jāgaraṇa* in the night and feeding of married *Brāmin* couples and girls—are important constituents of this vrata. Thus it is very costly affair.

13. *Caitra-Bhādrapada-Māgha Tṛtīyā Vratam:* It is observed by the laides or the girls on the days of *Śukla Tṛtīyā* of these three months. A *Manḍapa* should be constructed, and having taken, bath, wearing good cloths one must go to Devī temple.[322] This worship of *Gaurīs* prescribed with various kinds of flowers, fruits,s weat-meats, edibles, and cometies so on. In the night time, after every three hours—taking of bath and worship of Devi with *Homa* etc. is prescribed.[323] A functions hould be arranged in the night, dancing and singing must go on—as it pleases very much the goddess and the god *Śiva.*[324] Night is spent in gay mood in the company of the relatives, and the neighbours.Next day, the goddess is worshipped and donations are given to the *Brāhmiṇs,* ladies and food is served to all of them present there. This worship is performed in a temple and then the *Bhaktas* come to their own houses.[325]

14. *Gaurī Vratam:* On *Bhādrapada Kṛṣṇa Tṛtīyā, Gaurī* is worshipped in *Pañcapiñdika* form. Offering of *Dhūpa, Dīpa,* camphor, flowers, sweat-meats to the goddess feeding of the *Brāhmins* and the devotees of *Devī* is praised, and it gives good luck and wealth.[326]

15. *Manorath Tṛtīyā Vratam:* The *Caitra Śukla Tṛtīyā* is an auspicious day for the worship of *Viśvabhujā Devī* to obtain one's desires.[327] Goddess is having 20 hands,and performance of *Homa,* worship and offering of flowers and *Naivaidya* is made. In the end having observed it for one year on all the *Tṛtīyās, Paryṅka* with all the house-hold luxurious things is given to *Ācārya* and Twelve girls are to be fed. It is said that whatever the desire may be, it is fulfilled. This *Vrata* generally is performed in the night.

16. *Mangala Gaurī Vratam:* On *Caitra Śukla Tṛtīyā,* Mangala Gaurī is worshipped, and *Homa,* worship, feeding of girls, are performed.[328]

17. *Mahākāli Vratam:*[329] Generally on the night of *Kṛṣṇa Aṣṭhamī, Mahākāli* is worshipped with the offering of *Bali.* In the month *of Āśvina* on the 9th day also she is worshipped. Night awakening is said to be meritorious one.

18. *Gaurī Vratam:* This *Vrata* is observed on the day of *Māgha Śukla Caturthī* when *Gaurī* is worshipped. The ladies and gents worship her by offering *Kunda* flowers, red flowers, *Bali* and sweat-meats, milk, milk preparations and salty food preparations. Specially the ladies and the Brahmins are to be respected and food may be served to all the relatives and friends present there. This is to be celebrated every year by those who want prosperity and happiness in the life.

This *Vrata* may be called as *Dṇhunḍhi Vratam* or *Kunḍa Vratam or Śānti Vrata* and *Lalitā Vrata* also. The usual steps of worship like bathing of the deity, donations, recitaiton of the names of the deity, *Haven* etc. are to be performed.[330]

19. *Lalitikā Śaṣthī Vratam:* On the 6th day of bright fortnight of *Bhādrapada,* a lady should worship the goddess *Lalitikā*— a benign form of *Durgā*— with flowers, rice, *Naivaidya,* etc. In the night she should remain awakened and arrangements should be made for musical concernt, dancing by the courtesans, or by the house hold ladies *Kīrtan* may be performed. Next day Brahmins and the Virgin girls are to be fed and *Dakśinā* should be given. He or she receives all *Saubhāgya* and happiness in the life by performing this *Vrata.*[331] In the *Nārada Purāṇa* this *Saṣṭhi* is called *Chandan Saṣṭhi and Lalitā* is to be worshipped.[332] According to the *Nārada Purāṇa* this is also observed on Kṛṣṇa Saṣṭhi *and* and *Vrata* is called *Lalitā Vratam.*[333]

20. Kātyāyāni Saṣṭi Vratam: It is observed on *Śukla Saṣṭhi* of *Āśīvin* month[334] and *Devi Kātyāyani* is to be worshipped with auspitious things and, *Gandha* etc. Some say that *Durgā* is to be worshipped,[335] and Her image may be made of sand and in the end of *Vrata* the image may be thrown into the river. The laides of the Brāhmin family and girls are to be fed and respected with clothings and ornaments. By performing this a girl can obtain a good husband.

21. Mahāṣṭmi Vratam: 1. According to the *Nārada Purāṇa, Mahāṣṭamī is Vaiśākha Śāukla Aṣṭami.* The goddess *Aparājitā* is to be bathed and *Gandha, Kum Kum* etc. are offered, feeding of the girls and *Pārāṇa* is on *Navamī:* the devotee gets all his desires fulfiled.[336]

2. On *Jyeṣṭha Śukla-Aṣṭamī*—Devī is worshipped.[337]

3. On *Āṣādha Śukla Aṣṭami*—worship of Devī with *Pūjan-sāmagrī.*[338]

4. On *Śrāvaṇa Śukla Aṣṭami*—offering of sugar and milk.[339]

5. On *Māgha Kṛṣṇa Aṣṭamī—Bhadra Kālī* is worshipped[340]

6. On *Māgha Śukla Aṣṭaumī*—worship of *Devī* for the sake of progeny.[341]

7. On *Phālguna Kṛṣṇa Aṣtami*—worship of *Bhima-Devī.*[342]

8. *On* *Phālguṇa Śukla Aṣṭamī*—worship of *Śiva* and *Śiva* both,[343] as well as the worship of *Śhitala* with fried foods.[344]

9. On all the *Aṣṭamīs* of the year—*Śivā* and *Śiva* are worshipped.[345]

22. Dhvaja Navamī Vratam: On the day of *Śukla Navamī of* Pauṣa, the goddess *Kṛṣṇā*, the sister of *Kṛṣṇā* is worshipped. In this *Vrata* special feat is to install banners (*Dhvaja*) before the goddess, and in the *Devī* temple *Devī* is to be offered the flowers, *Gandha, Dhūpa* etc. and offer of the

Bali, full of meat, blood, wine and so on. Then feeding of the girls and *Kṣamāpaṇa* in the end, is perfromed. Who ever worships *Devī* with banners, he becomes free from all sorts of troubles and fears and is protected by the goddess.

23. Ulkā Navamī Vrata: It is supposed to be performed on the day on which *Devī* had killed demon *Mahiṣa.* The day falls in the month of *Āśvina* in *Śukla Pakṣa,* and *Devī* is to be worshipped with flowers and incense. Girssl are fed on this day and gifts of clothes and ornaments are given to them.[346]

24. Vir Navamī Vratam or Damanaka Navamī Vratam: The *Garuḍa Purāṇa* says that *Devī* should be worshipped on *Caitra Śukla Navamī* called *Vir Navamī or Damnaka Navamī.* On this day she is offered the flowers or garlands of Damnaka flowers. Then a devotee gets long age, health and prosperity as well as the power of destruction or subdueing his enemies.[347]

25. Śaurya Vratam: This *Vrata* is mentioned in the *Varāha Purāṇa* and is celebrated by the kings for the victory in the battles. In the month of *Āśvina* a devotee must make a mind to observe a *Vrata* on *Śukla Saptamī* and observe fast on *Aṣṭamī* and worship the goddess Durgā, and food should be offered to the Brāhmins. Having performed in this way for a year—at the end he must respect the girls with clothings, gold and food. In this way a devotee will be able, by the grace of the goddess, to regain even his lost kingdom and the cause of fear will be removed.[348]

26. Navamī Vratam: The *Viṣṇu Dharmottara Purāṇa* says that it is observed on all the *Śukla Navamīs* of the year in repect of *Bhadra Kālī,* starting from *Kārtika.* Every month the goddess is worshipped with *Gandha*, garland, *Dhūpa, Dīpa and Praśāda.* After one year, *Brāhmins* are to be fed, and clothings are given to them. The devotees become free of all sorts of troubles and fears caused by disease, theives, imprisonment, fire, decoits and the courts and obtain progeny, wealth, good wife and so on.[349]

27. Kokilā Vratam: This *Vrata* is to be observed by the ladies on the last day (*Pūrnimā*) of *Śrāvana.* Here the *Kokilā* is identified with the Goddess *Gaurī* or *Pārvatī,* who is to be worshipped with full devotion. Then the donations were given to the *Brāhmins,* the ladies were to be fed and *Dakśiṇā* given to them. The Ladies get good fate, and prosperity for the whole life.[350]

28. Bhūtamātā Utsava: The *Bhavisya Purāṇa* gives a story about the orign of *Bhūtamātā.* Here Kṛṣṇa says that she is orginated from the body of *Pārvati* while she was busy inconversation with *Śiva.*[351] This goddess looks after the welfare of the children and is worshipped all over India under different names, varying due to different actions, time, and place.[352] At the time of composition of this *Purāṇa,* the worshipe of *Bhūtamātā* was very popular and the people in the city as well as in the villages—celebrated a festival to respect her, with great enthusiasm.[353] This goddess, lives under an old tree and is worshipped by the people with water, flowers, lamps, food preparations (*Pūda, Lāpsi*) etc. She gives to her devotees, progeny, cattles, good health and protects the babies in the house from the *Śākins,* the demons and the *Grahas etc.*[354]

29. Vijayā Vratam: It is performed on the *Pūrnimā* of *Śrāvaṇa,*[355] for begeting the children, good fame, prosperity and health in the life, but it is specially meant for acquiring the kingdom, lost or new one. The Goddess may be worshipped in an image made of either gold, and silver, or sword. After performing *Havana,* and worship, *Naivaidya,* and clothings are offered. Donaitons to the priest, teacher, *Brāhmins,* and girls according to one's own capacity and liking are said to be meritorious.[356]

30. Pada Vratam: By the performance of *Pada Vrata* the goddess *Nandā,* is pleased. She is worshipped on an altar, an image, and Devī's foot-wear. The footwear made of gold etc. may be worshipped with mango-leaves, *Dūrvā*-grass, and *Bilva* leaves. Then donations and food should be offered to the girls and the devotees of Devī and in the end a person goes to *Devi Loka*. It was performed by *Prajāpāti, Vaśiṣṭha* and *Kaśyapa* etc.[357]

A study of these *Vratas* brings in light the following points about the cult of Sakti prevalent in the age of the *Purāṇas:*

1. That the Cult of *Śakti* was prevalent among the masses as a means to procure worldly luxuries and necessities—like progeny, good health, happienss, charming personality and last of all protection of the children.[358]

2. Generally these were the ladies who followed it, to procure good husband, to have good relations with their husbands, to subdue the co-wives, and to procure progeny and prosperity.[359]

3. It was the only cult which assured its devotees to protect from all the calamities, like fire, flood, draught, epics (*Mahāmārīs*), revolt in the states, enemy, and court-punishments, dense forest,dacoits and thieves etc.[360]

4. Except the *Durgā Pūjā* performed on *Āśīvna Śukla Navamī* and by the kings, the worship mostly was performed by the Right hand path. The steps *Bali*, and *Bhairavī Cakra* etc. were not performed, rather those were condemned in the *Purāṇas* and the aims to be achieved were also pertaining generally to the welfare side in the life. The *Saumya* forms of the goddess were more popular among the masses and some of these were worshipped as *Grāma deities.*

5. The *Śaktism* of the *Puraṇas* was concerned more with the personal life of its sectries and cared most with their protection in the life, homo-genity in the family and social relations, high-standards of living, observance of good and ethical behaviour, and last of all freedom from all the

dangers; and thus making them bold in the life.

Thus Śaktism was more or less, a social religion rather than an indiviudal cult. It believes in the reality of the universe, and teaches to have a faith and devotion towards the all loving mother-godoess.[361]

Foot Notes

1. Devi P. 1.55; 7.22. Dbh I.1.16; I.2.2; I .16.15; II.12.4 and so on. XII.13.26; XII.14.26.
2. Dbh. XI.1.21. See R.C. Hazra 'Upa-purāṇa Studies', Vol. II, p. 92,335.
3. *Ibid.* XI. 1.21-22.
4. *Ibid.* XI.1.24-29.
5. *Ibid.* XI.1.29-31.
6. Dbh. P.XI.8-13; XI. 16. 15-16.
7. *Ibid.* XI. 16.17;6.
8. *Ibid.* XI.13.26; XI.23,
9. *Ibid.* XI. 23 24-28.
10. *Ibid.* XII. 13. 3-4.
11. *Ibid.* XI.24.96-98.
12. *Ibid.* I.17.13-14. VII.39.26-30. XII.9.72-75;93;97;
13. *Ibid.*
14. Daśakumāra Charitam- I.57-58,p.32-35.
15. Devī p . 22.5; 24.19; 13.51b-52a.
16. Dbh. I.2.47.6-8.
17. Devī p. 93.262-265, Dbh.XII.9.59-63; VI.II.36-38.
18. Devī P.12.51; 22 5-6; 23-24.19; 88.4; 89.19; 91.1, 117.1-2. *Ibid.* 6.40.
19. *Ibid.* 7.95; 51.4-5.
20. *Ibid.* 121.5.
21. *Ibid.* 51.4-7.
22. *Ibid.* 34.3.
23. Nārada p. II.69.4-5.
24. Dbh. VI.17.6.
25. Devī P. 88.2-3.
26. Kalika p. 59. 185-186; 60-21-32. Devī p,99.p.143 of the Manuscript in Nāgarī script.
27. *Ibid.* 83.2-3.
28. Devī Purāṇa 90.5-8, Kalika p. 57.86-87.
29. *Ibid.* 90.9. Dbh. VII. 30. 85-101; vii.38.3.
30. *Ibid.* 117.7-9; 124. 1-2.
31. Devī p. 117.5.
32. *Ibid.* 45.5-18. Dbh. VII 33.39-42.
33. *Ibid.* 28.4-5.
34. Karmarkar, A.P., The Religions of India, Vol,I p, 197.
35. Dbh. VII. 39. 3-8; 34-47.
36. *Ibid.* VII. 40. 1-32; Kālikā p. 7.35 for yoga).
37. Clemen (Carl)- Religions of the world, p, 127. Devī p. 69.19.
38. Devi p. 124. 1 -13. Kālikā p. 66,17-19; 73.100-104.

Dbh.VI. 40,16-21; XI 18. 3-48.
39. Dbh XI. 17.35-47.
40. Dbh, IV 5.33; VII. 30. 93,
41. *Ibid.* IV 5.48-49.
42. *Ibid.* XI, 17 36; Kālikā p 24. 13, 1-30.
43. Mahābhāgavata p. 23.1-94; Kūrma p, 12.60-199. Lalitā Sahasra Nama of Brahmānda Purāṇa
44. Ibid. VI,13. 52, VI.II.61; VII 30.96-97.XII,9.61, Devī p. 93.261-264.
45. Widegrey (A.G.), The Comparative Study of Religions, p. 284.
46. Widegrey (A.G.) The comparative study of religions p. 284-85.
47. Devī P. 28.5; 33.48-109. Nārada P. I.123.73-75.
48. Devī P. 99.151; 79.1. Ch. 103-106.

Note: In this Purāṇa it is said that Devī is pleased by the offerings of cows to the Brāhmins, and full procedure for *Dhenu dana* prescribed.

49. Dbh. III.26.28-31. Kālikā P. 89.137-140.
50. *Ibid.* III.26.32.
51. Devī P. 28-3-9; 33..48-109; 59.1-3. Dbh. XI. 17.35-57; XI 18.1-70. Kālikā P. 59.1.94 62.43-48; 66-15-16-19; 72.27-28; 73.19-36; 56-800; 100-104; 74.1-55; 79.76-80.
52. Kālikā P. 59 161.
53. Devī P. 32.21-38.
54. Devā P. 32.32-34.
55. *Ibid.* 32.32.39.
56. *Ibid.* 50.20
57. *Ibid.* 50.18.
58. *Ibid.* 32.20.
59. *Ibid.* 50.32.
60. *Ibid.* 30.3-15.
61. *Ibid.* 30;2-17.
62. *Ibid.* 40.2.16.
63. Devī p. 32.4-5.
64. *Ibid.* 32.6.
65. *Ibid.*
66. *Ibid.* 32.7
67. *Ibid.* 32.9 Dbh X.8.6-24.13.30-32.
68. *Ibid.* 32.12-15.
69. Devi Bhāgavata P. VI.11.28. Devī p. 34-1-13.
70. Devī P. 34.9.13.
71. *Ibid.* 34.1-3
72. *Ibid* 34.4-8.
73. Devi P.118-1-22 1-8: movement of images to new temples, but not in North direction.15-22 Good results of this action.
74. *Ibid.* 102.3-4.
75. *Ibid.* 109.7-8.

76. *Ibid.* 102.5-7. 77. *Ibid.* 121.1-32.
78. *Ibid.* 79. *Ibid.*
80. Devī Purāṇa 91.9-82. See also Devī Bhāgavata Māhātmaya 5.67-68.
81. *Ibid.* 27.21. 82. *Ibid* 11; 26;21.
83. *Ibid.*5.3-5;27.25. 84. *Ibid.* 25.6,11.
85. *Ibid.* 26.9. 86. *Ibid.* 26.38.
87. *Ibid.* 26;21. 88. *Ibid.* 27.18.
89. Devī P. 27.26-57. 90. *Ibid.* 27.36; 25.
91. *Ibid.* 27.29a. 92. *Ibid.* 27.29-33.
93. Devī Bhāgavata V.11.45.
94. *Ibid.* VI.14.29. 95. *Ibid.* VI.14.26.
96. *Ibid* XII13.2-10.
97. Devī P. ch.31, Dbh. VII.38.45.
98. Devī P. 31.2-5, Bhāgavata P. 8.52.42.
99. Devī P. 31.6.8. 100. *Ibid.* 31.10-12.
101. *Ibid.* 31.14-15. 102. *Ibid.* 31.18-27.
103. *Ibid.* 31.28. 104. Devī Purāṇa 31,29.
105. *Ibid.* 31.30. 106. *Ibid.* 31.31.
107. *Ibid.* 31.32-41. 108. *Ibid.* 35.6
109. *Ibid.* 35.3. 110. *Ibid.* 35.a-10.
111. *Ibid.* 35.11, 19. 112. *Ibid.* 35.15.
113. *Ibid*, 35.16. 114. *Ibid.* 35.22-23.
115. Devī P. 35.29-33.
116. Dbh. III.27.4. Devī P, 35.17-18; 89.23;
117. *Ibid.* III.27.1-3. 118. *Ibid.* II. 27.5.
119. *Ibid.* III.27.6. 120. *Ibid.* III.27.7
121. *Ibid.* III.26.40. 122. Devī Bhagavata.III.26.
123. *Ibid.* III. 26.40-43. 124. *Ibid.* III. 26.40
125. *Ibid.* III. 26.45; 53.
126. *Ibid.* III. 26.46;54. 127. Ibid. III. 26.47; 55
128. *Ibid.* III. 26.51;56
129. Devī Bhagavata III.26,48; 57.
130. *Ibid.* III. 26.48; 58. 131. *Ibid.* III:26:49; 59.
132. *Ibid.* III. 26.50; 60. 133. *Ibid.* III. 26 .51.62.
134. *Ibid.* III. 26.52.62.
135. Devi P. 35.17-18. Devī Mahātmya XI.6.
136. Kane (P.V.) History of Dharma Śastra, Vol. V. pt. 1, p. 154. Mahābhāgavata P. 48 13-17. Bhaviṣya P.—Uttara Parva. 138, 1-115. Garuda P. 38.1-12.133.3-17; Agni P, 185.1-15 Nārada P.I.110.30-35.

137. Nirnayāmṛta p. 56.
138. Mārkaṇḍeya P. 89.11. Devī P. 21.13. Kālikā P. 88.9
139. Mārkaṇḍeya P. 89.1-15 Kālikā P. chs. 61-62 Devī Bhāgavata 3.26-27. Devī P. chs. 21-23. Māhābhāgavata. chs. 46 and 48 Varāha P. 28.41-48.
140. Kālikā P. 62.12-13, Māhābhagavata P. 69.19.
141. Devī P. 22.5; 23.3-5.
142. Devī P. 22.5-12.
143. Devi Māhātmya 12.12-15.
144. Bhaviṣya P. quoted by Pujā Prakash, p. 309. Māhābhāgavata P. 61, 12.13.
145. Devī P. 89.19
146. *Ibid.* 88.1-3.
147. *Ibid.* 22.6-7. See also—Mother goddess Kāmakhyā, Kākāti, p. 16-17.
148. Mahābhāgavata P. 46.15-20; Skanda P. and Bhaviṣya P. quoted in Tithi Tattva, p. 68.
149. Bhaviṣya P. quoted in Durgā-Bhakti Tarangini p. 20. Mahābhāgavata P. 45.1.
150. Devī Bh. 3.26.13-24.
151. Kālikā P. 62.18-20. Devī P. 89.1-25.
152. Devī Bh. 3.25.46.
153. Kālikā P. 62.28. Mahabhāgavata. P. 35 41-44. Devī P.22.10-12; 17-19.
154. Devī Bh. 3.36.7-35.
155. Kālikā P. 61.11-20 Mārkanḍeya P. 80.38.40. Matsya P. 260.56-66.
156. Devī Bh. 3.30.18-45. Devī P.22.11.
157. Brahma Vaivarta P.1.26.90-92 for Upacāras
158. Kālikā P. Chs. 72-73; and 61.26.28; 62.8-10. Devi P. 22.17-20.
159. Devī P. quoted by Kṛtya Ratnākara p. 35. Devī P. 22.12-15.Kālikā P. 63.14-15.
160. Kālikā P. ch. 71.3-5; 95-96.
161. *Ibid.* 71.96.97.
162. *Ibid.* 71.46-51; 112-113. Devī Bh. IX.30.78-81.
163. Kālikā P. 57.2-6.
164. *Ibid.* 71.20-23. Devī P. 22.15.
165. Kālikā P. 51.1.22; 71.105-112; 80.47-68. Devī P. 22.13-16.
166. *Ibid.* 71.39.

167. Kālikā P. 71.-6-18.57-58;
168. *Ibid.* 71-23-24.
169. Mahāhhāgavata P. 46 15-18. Guri Kalpa—quoted in the History of Dharma Śāstra, Vol. V. pt. I.p. 168 foonote. also Durgārchana Paddhati p. 671 Mahābhāgavata P. 48. 18-19.
170. Hemādri on Vrata, Vol. I, p. 909. Devī Bh. 3.26 32-33.
171. Kālikā P. 63. 16-19
172. *Ibid.* 22. 17; 35.17; 89.14; Skanda P. quoted by Hemdri Vol. I,p. 903.908.
173. Bhagavata 3.26.37-62. Devī P.22.19;91.15.
174. Devī Bh. 9.50 86.
175. Devī P. 55.1-10 76.43. Kāikā P. 63.38-39
176. Footnotes p. 171, History of Dharmasāśtrā, Vol. v. pt. 1
177. Kālikā P.88 9;, Mahābhāgavata P. 43.54-55. Devī Bh. 3.30.78-81.
178. Kālikā P. 61.88
179. Mārkanḍeya P.88.9. Devī Bh. VIII. 30.60, Mahābhāgavata P. 48.7
180. Devī P. quoted by Durgābhakti tarangini, p. 126.
181. Kālikā P. 6031; 62.20; 4,3; and quoted by Durgā Bhatriti Tarangini p. 21-22
182. History of Dharma Sastra, Vol. V. Pt. I. p. 177.
183. Devī P. 22.13-15. Devī Mahātmya 12.10 Kālikā P. 71.193. Devī Bh. 3.29.20.
184. Devī Bh. 3.26.32b-34.
185. Ibid. 3.26.32a.
186. Kālikā P. 71.49.51.
187. Devī P. 22.13-15.
188. Kālikā P. 57.2-6; 71.-5; 72.15-17.
189. Kālikā P. 71.18-19; 45; 139; 32.18; 71.73-89a.
190. *Ibid.* 57.4.71.153-168; 172-176;
191. *Ibid.* 71.96.-97.
192. *Ibid.* 71-46-48; 51; 5-6.
193. Yogini Tantra, 2.a.158.
194. *Ibid.* 2.7.170; 2.8.17. Kālikā P. 71.121.193.
195. Hunter: Statistical Account of Assam, 1879, Vol. II. p. 154.
196. Yogini Tantra, 2.5.156.

197. Devi Bh. 11.3.3; 11.7.40; 11.23 23-28.
198. Rigvedā 1.24. *Ibid.* Puruṣā Sukta, X. 90. Wilson R.V. 1, p. 60. Max Müller Ancient Skt. Literatnre, p. 408.
199. The Taittiriya Samhita, iii.4. Sānkhyayāna XVI.10-16. Satapatha Brh. XIII. iii.6.5.
200. Devi Bh. 8.23.10. Kālikā P. 71.18-19; 45; 139. Bhagavata P. V.9.13-15.
201. Asiatic Researches IV (Rep.), p. 371.Cosmo Publications, New Delhi.
202. Kālikā P. 71.80-83.
203. Kālikā P. 71.67-102.
204. *Ibid.* 71.20-46.
205. *Ibid.* 71.3.-7.
206. *Ibid.* 71.7.48.
207. *Ibid.* 71.18-19.
208. Harshacharita, p. 92.
209. Mālati Mādhavam—V.21-22 p. 229-232.
210. Kathāsaritsāgara, Crooke, Vol. II, p. 168.
211. Ghoshal U.M, Studies in Indian History and Culture, p. 479. Pāyne, The Sāktas, p. 13;
212. Mārkaṇḍeya P. 93.7-11. Devī Bhāgavata V. 35.28-29. Kālikā P.71.153-166.
213. Devī Māhātamya 13.9-12.
214. Kālikā P. 67.172, 184, 185.
215. *Ibid.* 13.14-18.
216. Tantrasāra, Bangabāsi ed., p. 983-34.
217. Prāṇatoshanī, p. 285.
218. Ghosnal (U.N.), Studies in Indian History and Culture p. 482.
219. Kālikā p. 67.50;71.51.
Tantrasāra, p. 934.
Haratattva Didhiti, p. 9. 329.
220. Ghoshal (U.N.). Studies in Indian History and Culture p. 481, 414 f.n.
221. Brāhatkathā Manjarī by Kshemen Ira, Hitopdesa III.8.
222. Bhagavata P. X.14.7.
Brīhaddharma P.III.42.17.
Devī P.474.
223. Brahma (N.K.), Philosophy of Hindu Sadhana, p 233.
224. Bhagavad Gītā, 2.44.
225. Devī P 4.74. Dbh. I. 12.51.VII. 39.10.47.

226. Dbh, II.18.58.
227. *Ibid.* VI. 22.56-57.VI. 14.14-15.
228. Devī Māhātmya 13.5.
229. Dbh. VI.5.25-27.VI.37.28;
230. Devī P. 5.74; Dbh. vi. 5.25-27,
231. Devī p. 7.6; 38. Dbh. VII. 37 .11-1?; IX.30.136-139.
232. Bṛahaddhama P. III.10.41-42.
233. Kālikā P. 60.3-28.
234. *Ibid.* 53.10; 59.104-105; 165 Dbh. VII. 37.15; 27.
235. Bhāgavādgīta 18.65-66.
236. Devī Māhātmya. XIII.7-18. Devī Bh. V.32, 35 chs. Brahma V.P. II.1.151. Śīva P. Uma Samhitā 5.451.
237. Dbh. III.30 18-60. Mahābhāgava P.chs chs. 36-48. Bṛahaddharma P. chs. 18 22.
238. Bhāgvata P. X Purvardha 22.1-5X Uttarardha 53.44-46.
239. Dbh. III. 12.66 III. 13-2-3;
240. Ibid. III. Ch. 15-23.
241. Devī Bh. III. 24.23-52; III.25.27-40.
242. *Ibid.* III.25.41-42.
243. Skanda P., Nāgara Khanda 177/6.
244. *Ibid.*—Kumārika Khanda (2) ch. 40.
245. *Ibid.* 5.3. Adh. 169. v.5.
246. Bhavisya P. 4.46.7.
247. Skanda, Prabhāsaksetra Ma, 58.29.
248. Bhavisva P.3.2.3; 34.
249. Kālikā P. 39. 163.
250. Bhaviṣya P. 3.1.3.
251. *Ibid.* 3.2.35.1.
252. Devi Bh VI.11.12.
253. Bhavisya, P. 9.5.1.
254. Ibid. 9.Adh. 15ff
255. Padma P. V.13.11-13, 18-34.
256. Brahmavaivarta, P. Ganeśakhanda, 36-42.
257. Devī P. 44.2-11. 82.47-48.
258. Kālikā P. chs. 8; 65-41.
259. Māhābhagāvata P. 56-32.
260. Dbh Xchs 1-13.
261. *Ibid.* IV.15.22-71
262. *Ibid* VI.8.50-70.
263. *Ibid* VII.27.1-40
264. *Ibid* VII 9.40-41
265. *Ibid.* IV. 5.33-50.
266. *Ibid.* I.15.1-60.
267. *Ibid.* 1.5.86-112.
268. *Ibid.* III 5.1-45.
269. *Ibid* I.7.15-50
270. *Ibid.* I 4.65

271. *Ibid.* IV 24.40-60. Varāha P. 160.33-75.
272. *Ibid.* X.6.1-6.
273. *Ibid.* IX.39.24-33.
274. Viśva Bandha Siddha Bhāratī p. 218.
275. Viśva Bandhā Siddha Bhāratī p. 221.
276. Bhaviṣya P., Uttara Parva, 16.1-16. Devī P. 23. 12-17.
277. *Ibid.* I. 122.13;27. Garuḍa P. 116/6
278. Bhavisya P. IV.134.67.
279. *Ibid.* IV.134.67. Garuda P.116.4
280. Bhaviṣya P. II.2.8/26
281. *Ibid.* 16.1-16. History of Dharm a Śāstra, Vol, v, pt I, p. 369.
282. Bhaviṣya I 21.1-30.
283. *Ibid.*, Uttara Parva, 121.36-37.
284. Dbh. VIII.24.45-57; 36.
285. Padma P. I.22.659. Matsya P. 62.4-5.
286. *Ibid.* I.20.51-52; 60-61.
Matsya P. p. 100.7-8; 15-16.
287. Nārada P. I.112-1-63; II.50.13-28.
288. Brh. V.P. IV. 27.122-123.
289. Padma P. I.22.70-72; 78.
290. *Ibid* I.22.90-100.98, 84. Matsya P. 62.4-39.
291. Padma P. I.22.85-88. Matsya P. 62.22-25
292. Nārada P. I.112.1-9. History of Dharma Sastra, Vol;. V. pt I, p. 296.
293. Bhaviṣya P. Uttar Parva 121-154-156. Padma P. I.20.103-104
294. Padma P. I.21.141-143. Matsya P. 100.53.
295. Brahma Vaivarta Purāṇa IV.27.2-50.
296. Bhaviṣya P., Uttara Parva 23.1-28. History of Dharma śāstra, Vol. V. pt I, p. 277,
297. *Ibid.* Uttara Parva 23.12.
298. Skanda p. Brahmottara Khanda, 18.25-70.
299. Agni Purāṇa 199.9
300. Bhaviṣya P., Uttar Parva 24.1-36.
301. *Ibid.* 18.1-36.
302. *Ibid.* 27.1-27.
303. *Ibid.* 27.5.13
304. Matsya P. 64.1-26.
305. Padma P. I.22.136-164.
306. Padma P. I.22.161.
307. *Ibid.* 122.160
308. Bhaviṣya Purāṇa Uttar Parva 26.1-41; Padma P. I.22.105

History of Dharma Sāstra Vol. V, pt I., p 390.
309. Matṣya Purāṇa 63.2.-
310. *Ibid.* 63.23-25.
311. *Ibid.* 63.15-17.
312. *Ibid.* 63.4-11.
313. Bhavisya P. Uttara Parva, 20.1-28. Nārada Purāṇa I.II23-36.
314. Bhaviṣya P. Uttara parva 25.1-44, Matṣya P. 60.14-49.
315. *Ibid* 25.31-32.
316. Agni P. '178-1-28.
317. Padma P. 12.9.10.58.
318. Bhaviṣya P. Uttar Parva, 21.1-44.
319. Bhaviṣya P. Uttar Parva 22.1-36.
320. *Ibid.* 22.12-18.
321. Ibid. 29.1-77.
322. Bhaviṣyā P. Uttar Parva, 28.15-16.
323. *Ibid* 28.1-20.
324. *Ibid.* 28.29.
325. *Ibid.* 28-1-58.
326. Skanda P. 6.168;25-77.
327. Ibid. IV-2.80.1-86
328. Skanda P IV.1;49, 55-91.
329. *Ibid.* 7.130.1-12.
330. Nārada Purṇa I, 113.80-86.
331. Bhaviṣya P., Uttar Pārva 41.1-181.
332. Nārada P. I.115.29-30.
Gutpa (B.A.) Hindu Holidays and Ceremonials, p. 78-82.
333. Nārada P. I.115.8-15.
334. Narada P. I.115.34-37.
335. Gupta (B.A.) Hindu Holidays and Ceremonials, p. 75.
336. Nārada P. 1.117.4-7
337. *Ibid.* I.117,8-9.
338. *Ibid.* I.117.9-12.
339. *Ibid* I.117,13-14.
340. *Ibid.* I.118,90.
341. Nārada P. I.118.91.
342. *Ibid.* 1.118.92.
343. *Ibid.* I.118.93.
344. *Ibid.* I.118.94-98.
345. *Ibid.* I.118.99.
346. Agrawal (V.S.), Matsya Purāṇa, a Study, P.156.
347. Garuḍa Purāṇa, 135/2, 5.
348. Varāha Purāṇa 64.2-6
349. Viṣṇu Dharmottar Purāṇa III.178.1-5
350. Nārada P. I.124.19-25.
351. Bhaviṣya Purāṇa 134.4-18.

352. Bhaviṣya Purāṇa 136.25,
353. *Ibid.* 136 1.
354. *Ibid.* 136.20-23
355. Devi P. 100,4-15; 26.
356. *Ibid.* 102.10-13.
357. *Ibid*, 102-14-
358. Devī P. 93.261-264; Davī Bhāgvata III. 25.43-46 XII.9.59-63.
359. Ibid.
360. Vāyū P. 9.95-96. Devi Bh. Mahatmya 3.41-47, 5.90-91.
361. Devī Mahatmya 13.36, 37; Murti Rahasya V.24.

four

Śāktism, or Goddess-Worship

Śāktism in the simplest acceptation of the term is the worship of power or force (Sanskṛit *Śakti*) personified as a goodess, with a view to the acquisition of magical and supernatural faculties through her help, or to the distruction of enemies through her co-operation.

Of course it is alleged by all Śaiva and Vaishṇava sectarians that the gods Śiva and Vishṇu, as identified with the Supreme Being, are themselves the source and spring as well as the controllers of all the forces and potentialities of nature. Yet we must bear in mind that it is a rooted idea with all Hindū theologians, of whatever donomination, that the highest condition of the Self-existent Being is a condition of complete quiescence and inactivity, as well as of complete oneness, solitariness, and impersonality.

In fact the theory of Brāhmanism, as we have seen, is that the one Self-existent Being is abstract Spirit, and that that Spirit is Life without anything to live for, Thought without anything to think about, Joy without anything to be joyful about. But the moment this one Self-existent pure Spirit begins to be conscious of existence—to exercise thought and feel joy—it assumes personality and material organization. It becomes, in fact, a personal God; and when this personal God wills to put forth energy for the creation of a world external to himself his nature becomes duplex. Of course the absolute unity and strictly masculine character of that nature might have been preserved in his personal development, but the idea of a kind of duality in unity very soon suggested itself to the Hindū mind. He was held to possess a double nature, partly male and partly female, the female constituting his left side.

Then, again, this duality might have been evenly balanced, or the preponderance of active faculties might have been assigned, in accordance with European ideas, to the male side. We find, however, that the Hindūs, in dividing the divine nature into two halves, formed no idea of any due co-ordination of working power between them as between man and woman. On the contrary, the male side of the god was believed to relegate all his more onerous and troublesome executive functions to his female counterpart. And hence it has come to pass that the female side of the personal god is often more honoured and propitiated than the male. Hence it is that the worshipper is inclined to turn with greater devotion to the goddess than to the god when he supplicates any powerful intervention on his own behalf in circumstances of unusual exigency or peril.

This I believe to be the true theory of Śāktism in its simplest and most general aspect. It is a theory which is certainly more closely connected with Śaivism than with any other system. Like Śaivism, too, it traces back its origin to philosophical Brāhmanism, and through Brāhmanism to the earliest conceptions foreshadowed in the Veda.

Perhaps the first dawn of the idea of duality in unity is to be found in the well-known 29th hymn of the 10th Maṇḍala of the Ṛig-veda, already quoted. In that hymn we find it stated that in the beginning when there was neither entity nor nonentity—when in fact the universe was about to be developed—there arose in the One Being Desire which produced Mind and all existing things.

But the idea of a universe proceeding from a female principle brought into union with a male is more fully developed in other Vedic texts.

Probably Heaven (Dyaus) and Earth (Pṛithivī) are the most ancient of all Vedic gods, and from their fancied union as husband and wife the other deities and the whole Universe were at first supposed to spring. They are often described as parents (janitrī, Ṛig-veda X. 110. 9; pitarā, III. 3. 11; mātarā, I. 155. 3). Or Heaven alone is called father (pitā) and Earth mother (mātā). On the other hand, elsewhere in the Veda the female deity Aditi—probably a personification of the sky or of universal nature—seems to stand alone, taking the place of both Heaven and Earth as parent of the dieties, her counterpart being Diti the mother of the demons. Another important goddess in the Ṛig-veda is the Dawn (Ushas,'Hες[1]), the Sky's daughter, who is of course closely connected with the Sun-god; but is not described as married to him, though followed by him as a lover is pursued by his mistress.

And here it may be noted as remarkable that the wives of two chief Vedio gods, Indra and Agni (Indrāṇī and Agnāyī), are not associated with their husbands or exalted to equal rank as objects of worship. Nor is the popular goddess Lakshmī, afterwards wife of Vishṇu, mentioned at all in the Ṛig-veda[2]. Nor is Sarasvatī held to be the consort of Brahmā. She is rather a river-goddess, though often invoked in other characters, and once associated with a river-god Sarasvat (VII. 96. 4, 6). It is only when we come to the Brāhmaṇas and Upanishads that we find the duality of the divine nature clearly enunciated. For example, in the Śatapatha-Brāhmaṇa (XIV. 4. 2. 1), before noticed, and Bṛihad-āraṇyāka Upanishad (III. 1) we read to the following effect: 'The One Being did not enjoy happiness when alone. He was desirous of a second. He divided himself into two. Hence were husband

and wife produced. Therefore was this (second) only a half of himself as the half of a split pea is.' It is then related how all beings were produced by the union of the divine male and divine female. Śaṅkara, in his comment on the Upanishad, observes, in relation to the above passage, 'Because this male half is void as wanting the female half, therefore after taking a wife it is completed by the female half as a split pea is by being joined with its other half' (see Roër's translation).

If we pass on to Manu, we find that the Self-existent is described as dividing his own substance and becoming half male and half female (I. 5, etc.).

Turning next to the Vedānata and Sāṅkhya philosophical systems, we know that they teach the separate existence of eternal Spirit called 'the Self' or 'Male' on the one side and of an eternal productive force or prolific germ (Māyā or Prakṛiti fem.) on the other. The union of the two was believed to be indispensable before any creation could result.

Of course ordinary thinkers gave a concrete reality to all such metaphysical speculations. The Spirit—which was called 'the Self' (Ātman) in one system and 'the Male' (Purusha) in the other—became in the popular creed a separate male god, while the productive prolific force became a separate female god. The union of the two was expressed in the later mythology by the Ardha-nārī or androgynous form of Śiva—in which one half or the right side of the god's person is represented as male and the other half or left side as female—or more commonly by the male and female symbols (the Liṅga and Yoni) set up in innumerable shrines throughout every part of India.

The same doctrine is constantly repeated in the Purāṇas; but even in those writings, or at least in those of them which are considered orthodox, it is to be noted that although they often countenance and even promote Śākta views by making the active power of the goddess a subject of special laudation, and by according greater honour to the female deity (as for example in placing the goddess first in such compounds as Lakshmī-Nārāyaṇau, Sītā-Rāmau, Rādhā-Kṛishṇau[3]), yet no exclusive or extravagant worship of the goddess in inculcated.

It was reserved for the latest sacred writings called Tantras to identify all Force with the female principle in nature, and to teach an undue adoration of the wives of Śiva and Vishṇu to the neglect of their male counterparts.

Practically, as we shall see, the Śāktism of the present day is a mere offshoot of Śaivism. It ineulcates an exclusive adoration of Śiva's wife as the source of every kind of supernatural faculty and mystic craft. This, in fact, is the central doctrine and leading idea of all Tāntrik writings. For the Tantras, believed as they are to be a direct revelation from Śiva to his wife Pārvatī, are the bible of Śāktism just as the Purāṇas are the bible of ordinary Śaivism and Vaishṇavism[4]. That they are regarded by some as of equal divine authority with the Puràṇas, and even as a kind of secondary revelation, is evident from a passage in Kullūka's commentary on Manu II. 1. There he asserts that divine truth is of two kinds; namely, 'that revelated in the Vedas and that found in the Tantras.' It is certain that a vast proportion of the mhabitants of India, especially in Bengal, are guided in their daily life by Tāntrik teaching, and are in bondage to the gross superstitions inculcated in these writings.

And indeed it can scarcely be doubted that Śāktism is Hindūism arrived at its worst and most corrupt stage of development. To follow out the whole process of evolution would not be easy. Suffice it to say that just as Hindūi sm resolved itself into two great systems—Śaivism and Vaishṇavism—so the adherents of those two systems respectively separated into two great classes. The first are now called 'followers of the right-hand path' (Dakshiṇa-mārgīs). These make the Puraṇ as their real Veda (nigama), and are devoted to either Śiva or Vishṇu in their double nature as male and female. But they do not display undue preference for the female or left-hand side of the deity; nor are they addicted to mystic or secret rites. The Second class are called 'followers of the left-hand path' (Vāma-mārgīs) : these make the Tantras their own peculiar Veda (āgama), tracing back their doctrines to the Kaula Upanishad, which is held to be the original authority for their opinions; whence their system is sometimes called Kaula, as well as Śākta, and they themselves Kaulikas.

And it is these left-hand worshippers who, I repeat, devote themselves to the exclusive worship of the female side of Śiva and Vishṇu[5]; that is, to the goddess Durgā or Kālī (=Ambā, Devī) rather than to Šiva; to Rādhā rather than to Kṛishṇa; to Sītā rather than to Rāma; but above all to Ambā or Devī, the mother-goddess, identified with Śiva's consort, but regarded in her most comprehensive character as the great Power (Śakti) of Nature, the one Mother of the Universe (Jagan-mātā, Jagad-ambā)—the mightly mysterious Force, whose function is to direct and control two quite distinct operations; namely, first, the working of the natural appetites and passions, whether for the support of the body by eating and drinking, or for the propagation of living organisms through sexual cohabitation; secondly, the acquisition of supernatural faculties and magical powers (siddhi), whether for a man's own individual exaltation or for the annihilation of his opponents.

And here it is necessary to observe that the Śākta form of Hindūism is equipped with a vast mythological Personnel of its own—an immense array of female personalities, constituting a distinct division of the Hindū Pantheon.

Yet the whole array, spreading out as it does into countless ramifications, has its root in the wife of Śiva. By common consent she is held to be the source or first point of departure of the entire female mythological system. She also stands at its head; and it is remarkable that in every one of the male god Śiva's characteristics, his consort is not only his counterpart, but a representation of all his attributes intensified. We have already pointed out how it came to pass that the male god gradually gathered under his own personality the attributes and functions of all other divinities, and thus became to his own special worshippers the great god (Mahā-devaḥ) of Hindūism. Similarly and in a much greater degree did his female counterpart become the one great goddess (Mahā-devī) of the Śākta hierarchy; representing in her own person all other female manifestations of Brahmā, Vishṇu, and Śiva, and absorbing all their functions. For this reason even the wives of Brahmā and Vishṇu were said to be her daughters. As to the opposite and contradictory qualities attributed to her, these are no source of difficulty to a Hindū mind. She is simply in all respects a duplicate of her husband, but a duplicate painted in deeper or more vivid colours.

And just as Śiva is at one time white (Śveta, śukla) both in complexion and character, at another black (Kāla); so his female nature also became one half white (whence one of her names Gaurī) and the other half black (whence her name Kālī).

Then, again, each of these opposite characters became variously modified and endlessly multiplied. The white or mild nature ramified into the Śaktis called Umā, Gaurī, Lakshmī, Sarasvatī, etc.; the black or fierce nature into those called Kālī, Durgā, Caṇḍī, Cāmuṇḍā, etc. And just as Śiva has 1008 names or epithets, so his wife possesses a feminine duplicate of nearly every one of his designations. At least one thousand distinct appellations are assigned to her, some expressive of her benignant, some of her ferocious character. Notably it is declared in the Tantras that if any one repeats eight of her names containing the letter *m*, kings will become his servants, all men will love him, and all his difficulties come to a happy termination.

In short, all the other Śaktis came to be included by the Śāktas under the Śakti or female energy of Śiva, which eventually developed into innumerable separate manifestations and personifications.

These personifications, following the analogy of some of Vishṇu's incarnations, are somethimes grouped according to a supposed difference of participation in the divine energy, such for example as the full energy (pūrṇā śakti), the partial (anśarūpiṇī), the still more partial (kalā-rūpiṇī), and the partial of the partial (kalānśa-rūpiṇī), this last including mortal women in various degrees, from Brāhman women downwards, who are all worshipped as forms of the divine mother manifesting herself upon earth; for it must not be forgotten that in the Śàkta creed every female is a present divinity.

The more usual classification, however, begins with the Mahā-vidyās. These are held to be ten in number, that number being probably selected to match the ten chief incarnations of Vishṇu. They are called Mahā-vidyās as sources of the goddess's highest knowledge; that is to say, of the knowledge which confers preternatural powers. They have all different attributes, and are thus designated:—1. Kālī (sometimes called Śyāmā), black in colour, fierce and irascible in character. 2. Tārā, a more benign manifestation, worshipped especially in Kaśmīr. 3. Shoḍaśī, a beautiful girl of sixteen (also called Tripurā, worshipped in Malabar). 4. Bhuvaneśvarī. 5. Bhairavī. 6. Chinna-mastakā, a naked goddess holding in one hand a blood-stained scimitar and in the other her own severed head, which drinks the warm blood gushing from her headless trunk. 7. Dhūmavatī, 'in the form of smoke.' 8. Vagalā or Bagalā, 'having the face of a crane.' 9. Mātāṇgī, 'a woman of the Bhaṅgī caste.' 10. Kamalātmikā. Of these the first two are especially Mahā-vidyās, the next five Vidyās, and the last three Siddha-vidyās.

The next class of personifications or manifestations of the goddess are the Mātṛis or Mātṛikās (or Mahā-mātṛis), the great mothers of the Universe. These are more important than the Mahā-vidyās in their connexion with the prevalence of Mother-worship, a form of religion which, among the peasantry of India. often takes the place of every other creed. This will be more fully explained in the chapter on tutelary deities (p. 209).

The Mātṛis or Mothers are—1. Vaishṇavī. 2. Brāhmī or Brahmāṇī, often represented with four faces or heads like the god Brahmā. 3. Kārttikeyī, sometimes called Māyūrī. 4. Indrāṇī. 5. Yāmī. 6. Vārāhī, connected with the boar incarnation of Vishṇu. 7. Devī or Īśānī, represented with a trident in one hand as wife of Śiva. 8. Lakshmī[6]. Each of these divine Mothers is represented with a child in her lap.

Closely related to the Mothers is a class of female personifications called the eight Nāyikās or mistresses. These, of course, are not necessarily mothers. In fact no other idea is connected with them than that of illegitimate sexual love. They are called Balinī, Kāmeśvarī, Vimalā, Aruṇā, Medinī, Jayinī, Sarveśvarī, and Kaulesī.

Another class of manifestations is that of the Yoginīs. These are sometimes represented as eight fairies or sorceresses created by and attendant on Durgā, sometimes as mere forms of that goddess, sixty or sixty-five in number, and capable of being multiplied to the number of ten millions.

Other classes not worth enumerating are the Ḍākiṇīs and Śakinīs. These are simply female fiends or orgresses of most repulsive habits, and are not so much manifestations of the goddess as impish servants always attendant on her.

But it is in the form Kālī—the form under which the

goddess is worshipped at Calcutta—that she is most terrible.

The following is a free translation of two passages in the Tantras descriptive of Kālī's appearance[7]:—

'One should adore with liquors and oblations that Kālī who has a terrible gaping mouth and uncombed hair; who has four hands and a splended garland formed of the heads of the giants she has slain and whose blood she has drunk; who holds a sword in her lotus-like hands; who is fearless and awards blessings; who is as black as the large clouds and has the whole sky for her clothes; who has a string of skulls round her neck and a throat besmeared with blood; who wears ear-rings (consisting of two dead bodies); who carries two dead bodies in her hands; who has terrible teeth and a smiling face; whose form is awful and who dwells in burning-grounds (for consuming corpses); who stands on the breast of her husband Mahā-deva[8].'

'A Kaulika (*i.e.* a Śākta) should worship Kālī, who lives amongst dead bodies; who is terrible and has fearful jaws; who has uncombed hair and a glowing tongue; who constantly drinks blood; who stands over her husband Mahākāla[9] and wears a garland of skulls on her blood-besmeared throat; who has prominent breasts; who is waited on by all the Siddhas as well as by the Siddhīs.'

It is this goddess who thirsts for blood, and especially for human blood; and if the blood of animals is not offered to her, she takes that of men. In one of the Tantras kings are directed to appease her by the sacrifice of human beings (nara-bali). The blood of a tiger is said to satisfy her for 100 years, and that of a man for 1000 years.

It might have been expected that a creed like this, which admits of an infinite multiplication of female deities and makes every woman an object of worship, would be likely to degenerate into various forms of licentiousness on the one hand and of witchcraft on the other. But if such consequences might have been anticipated, the actual fact has been worse than the most gloomy possimist could possibly have foretold. In Śāktism we are confronted with the worst results of the worst superstitious ideas that have ever disgraced and degraded the human race. It is by offering to women the so-called homage of sensual love and carnal passion[10], and by yielding free course to all the grosser appetites, wholly regardless of social rules and restrictions, that the worshippers of the female power (Śakti) in Nature seek to gratify the goddess representing that power, and through her aid to acquire supernatural faculties, and even ultimately to obtain union with the Supreme Being. Incredible as it may appear, these so-called worshippers actually affect to pride themselves on their debasing doctrines, while they maintain that their creed is the grandest of all religions, because to indulge the grosser appetites and passions with the mind fixed on union with the Supreme Being is believed to be the highest of all pious achievements. Indeed; according to the distorted ideas and perverted phraseology of the sect, all who are uninitiated into this system are styled 'beasts' (paśu[11]), the initiated being called Siddha, 'the perfect ones.'

The rite of initiation (Dīkshā) must be performed by a proper Guru or teacher, who does little more than impart a knowledge (upadeśa) of certain mystic texts and syllables to the candidate, but the rite ought never to take place unless moon, planets, and stars are favourable. If a pupil can be initiated during the occurrence of a solar eclipse wonderful advantages may be expected to accrue to both teacher and taught.

Of course, the principal rites, or rather orgies, of Śākta worshippers take place in secret and with closed doors. This secrecy is strictly in accordance with Tāntrik precept. Thus, we read:—

'One should not practise the Kaula system in the presence of the uninitiated (Paśus or beasts), any more than one should recite the Veda in the presence of a Śūdra.

'One should guard the Kaula system from the Paśus just as one guards money and grain and clothes from thieves.

'One should conceal the Kaula system like the water in the cocoa-nut; one should be a Kaula internally, a Śaiva externally, and a Vaishṇava when talking at public meetings.

'The Vedas, the Śāstras, and the Purāṇas are clearly like a common woman (open to all), but this mystical Śaiva science is like a high-born woman (kept secluded).'

Hence no one who has been initiated into the practices of the sect can be persuaded to speak of them to the uninitiated. Probably the spread of education and the influence exercised by Christian men and women throughout India is gradually operating to abolish all the grosser forms of Śāktism, as they have already helped to do away with Satī, female infanticide, human sacrifices, and other monstrous evils. Still it is well known that even in the present day, on particular occasions, the adherents of the sect go through the whole ceremonial in all its revolting entirety. When such occasions occur, a circle is formed composed of men and women seated side by side without respect of caste or relationship [12]. Males and females are held for the particular occasion to be forms of Śiva and his wife respectively, in conformity with the doctrine propounded in one of the Tantras, where Śiva addressing his wife says, 'All men have my form and all women thy form; any one who recognizes any distinction of caste in the mystic circle (Cakra) has a foolish soul.'

The actual performance of the ceremonial then follows. It consists of five separate actions:—1. The drinking of wine and liquors of various kinds (madya); 2. the eating of meat (mānsa); 3. the eating of fish (matsya); 4. the eating of parched or fried grain (mudrā); 5. sexual union (maithuna)[13].

With regard to the first four of these acts the Tantras prescribe twelve sorts of liquors, three sorts of wine, and three sorts of meat. Pulastya, one of the ancient sages who are the supposed authors of certain law-books, also enumerates twelve kinds of liquors, as follows:—1. liquor extracted from the bread-fruit (panasa), called Jack-liquor; 2. from grapes (drākshā); 3. from date-palm (kharjūrī); 4. from common palm (tālī), or toddy; 5. from coco-nut (nārikela); 6. from sugar-cane (ikshu); 7. from the Mādhvīka plant; 8. longpepper liquor (saira); 9. soap-berry liquor (arishṭa); 10. honey liquor (mādhūka); 11. a kind of rum or liquor prepared from molasses, etc. (called Gauḍī, or sometimes Maireya); 12. arrack, or liquor prepared from rice and other grain (surā, or vāruṇī, or paishṭī).

Besides the above twelve kinds of spirituous drink others are frequently mentioned; for example, Ṭāṅka, made from wood-apple; Koli, made from the jujube; and Kādambarī; the last being the favourite beverage of Bala-rāma.

The meat may be that of birds, beasts, or fish. The parched grain is eaten, like dry biscuit, as a relish with the wine and spirituous liquors. The drinking of each kind of drink is supposed to be attended with its own peculiar merit and advantage. Thus one liquor gives salvation, another learning, another power, another wealth, another destroys enemies, another cures diseases, another removes sin, another purifies the soul.

The Mātṛikā-bheda Tantra (quoted by Dr. Rajendralāla Mitra) makes Śiva address his own wife thus:—'O sweet-speaking goddess, the salvation of Brāhmans depends on drinking wine. I impart to you a great truth, O mountainborn, when I say that the Brāhman who devotes himself to drinking and its accompaniments, forthwith becomes a Śiva. Even as water mixes with water, and metal blends with metal; even as the confined space in a pitcher merges into the great body of surrounding space on the destruction of the confining vessel, and air mingles with air, so does a Brāhman melt into Brahmā, the universal soul.

'There is not the least doubt about this. Likeness to the divinity and other forms of beatitude are designed for Kshatriyas and others; but true knowledge can never be acquired without drinking spirituous liquor; therefore should Brāhmans alwasy drink. No one becomes a Brāhman by repeating the Gāyatrī, the mother of the Vedas; he is called a Brāhman only when he has knowledge of Brahma. The ambrosia of the gods is their Brahma, and on earth it is arrack (or liquor distilled from rice); and because one attains through it the condition of a god (suratva), therefore is that liquor called surā.'

It is not surprising, therefore, that in Bengal some respectable mothers of families, who believe the above passage to be a direct revelation from Śiva and who would not dream of drinking spirits for their own gratification, never say their prayers without touching their tongues with a pointed instrument dipped in arrack, and never offer flowers to their god without sprinkling them with a few drops of that liquor.

In short, the drinking of spirituous liquor is as much an essential part of the Śākta ceremonial as the drinking of Soma juice was of the Vedic sacrifices, and the drinking of arrack (surā) was of the Sautrāmaṇi and Vājapeya and other sacrificial rites. Indeed these ancient rites are appealed to in the Tantras as a justification for the Śākta practice.

Nor can there be any doubt that a one time the drinking of wine and spirituous liquors was universal all over India[14]. Some of the gods were supposed to set the example—notably Śiva [15] with his wife Durgā, and Balarāma elder brother of Kṛishṇa with his wife Revatī—and we find that one of the products of the ocean when churned by the gods and demons was Surā, or spirit distilled from rice, and that one of the seven seas encircling the earth was believed to be composed entirely of that liquor[16]. Drunkenness in fact became such an evil that to remedy it a kind of temperance movement appears to have been eventually organized, leading to a complete reaction to the other extreme of total abstinence. Hence we find that in Manu's time the penalty for drinking spirits was to commit suicide by drinking them when in a boiling state (XI. 91).

In the same way the eating of meat was once universal in India; cows were sacrificed[17] and the flesh eaten, especially at Śrāddhas, where the aroma of beef was thought to be an excellent aliment for the spirits of the dead. Manu allows all sorts of animal food to be eaten, provided that small portions are first offered to the gods and to the spirits of departed ancestors (V. 32); and Vālmīki, when he entertained Vasishṭha at his hermitage (as described in the Uttara-Rāma-caritra), regaled him with the 'fatted calf.' The Śāktas, therefore, have good ground for asserting that in drinking wine and eating meat they are merely reverting to the practice of their ancestors. Yet it is curious that they think it necessary to go through the form of neutralizing the curse of the great Śukra Ācārya (see note, p.194) before beginning their potations. This they do by repeating three particular Mantras and certain magical formulæ, after drawing a triangle on the ground with the finger dipped in spirituous liquor.

The fifth act of the Śākta ceremonial—the union of the actual man and woman—is held to be the most important of all. In the minds of some it is supposed to symbolize a great cosmical mystery—the production of the universe through the union of Purusha and Prakṛiti (see pp.30, 31)—a mystery constantly kept before the mind by the worship of the two stone symbols Liṅga and Yoni.

'The only salvation,' says a Tantra, 'is that which results from spirituous liquors, meat, and cohabitation with women.'

The holy circle (śrī-cakra) or meeting of the members of the sect on solemn occasions (represented by a mystical diagram) is said to be 'the door to the highest form of salvation—complete union with the Supreme Being (sāyujya-mukti).'

These circles are of different kinds according to the difference in the rank, character, and occupation of the women (śaktis) present at them. Thus there is the Vīra-cakra, the Mahā-cakra, the Deva-cakra, the Rāja-cakra, etc.

It is to be observed, however, that all the five acts we have described do not necessarily take place at every meeting.

Moreover, besides the five so-called ceremonial acts performed by Śāktas at their secret meetings, there are six other methods of propitiating the goddess with a view to acquire superhuman powers (siddhi)—namely, by the use of Mantras, Bījas (or Vījas), Yantras, Kavacas, Nyāsas, and Mudrās.

The subject of the employment of Mantras or sacred texts, their use, misuse, and prostitution to the worst purposes, is one of the greatest interest and importance in its bearing on the past and present religious condition of the Hindūs.

A Mantra, as most persons know, is properly a divinely inspired Vedic text, but with the Śāktas, and indeed with the great mass of the Hindūs in the present day, it loses this character and becomes a mere spell or charm. Even though the text be taken from the Ṛig, Yajur or Atharva-veda (p. 8), and be generally employed as a prayer or invocation with a definite meaning and application attached to the words, it becomes with the Śāktas a mere collection of magical letters and sounds, which, if properly uttered and repeated according to prescribed formularies, possesses in itself a mystical power capable of causing every conceivable good to one's self or evil to one's enemies.

The Bījas, again, are mystical letters or syllables invented for the sake of brevity to denote the root (mūla) or essential part of such Mantras, or the name of the deity to whom it may be addressed, or some part of the body over which that deity presides. For example:—*Am* is said to denote Śiva, *U* Vishṇu, *Hrim* the sun, *Lam* the earth, *Nam* the mind, *Dham* both the goddess Bhuvaneśvarī and the tongue, *Nam* both the goddess Annapūrṇā and the nose, *Pam* the ear, etc.

Perhaps the following abridgment of a passage from a little work by Pratāpa-candra Ghosha descriptive of the worship of Durgā (Durgā-pūjā) in Bengal, and giving directions for the performance of a preparatory rite called Bhūta-śuddhi, removal of evil demons,' will give the best idea of the uses to which the Bījas are applied:—

> Holding a scented flower, anointed with sandal, on the left temple, repeat *Om* to the Gurus, *Om* to Gaṇeśa, *Om* to Durgā. Then with *Omphat* rub the palms with flowers, and clasp the hands thrice over the head, and by snapping the fingers towards ten different directions, secure immunity from the evil spirits. Next utter the Mantra *Ram*, sprinkle water all around, and imagine this water as a wall of fire. Let the priest identify himself with the living spirit (jīvātman) abiding in man's breast, in the form of the tapering flame of a lamp, and conduct it by means of the Sushumṇā nerve through the six spheres within the body upwards to the Divine spirit. Then meditate on the twenty-four essences in nature; *viz*. the Producer, Intellect, Egoism, the five subtle and five gross elements, the five external organs of sense, the five organs of action, with mind. Conceive in the left nostril the Mantra *Yam*, declared to be the Bīja or root of wind; repeat it sixteen times while drawing air by the same nostril; then close the nose and hold the

breath, and repeat the Mantra sixty-four times.

Then meditate on the Mātṛikā, and say, 'Help me, goddess of speech:' *Am* to the forehead, *Am* to the mouth, *Im* to the right eye, *Im* to the left eye, *Um* to the right ear, *Um* to the left ear, *Im* to the right cheek, *Im* to the left cheek, *Em* to the upper lip, *Aim* to the lower lip, *Om* to the upper teeth, *Aum* to the lower teeth, *Tam*, *Tham*, *Dam*, *Dham*, and *Nam* to the serveral parts of the left leg, *Pam* to the right side, *Pham* to the left, *Bam* to the back, *Mam* to the stomach, *Yam* to the heart, *Ram* to the right shoulder, *Lam* to the neck-bone, *Vam* to the left shoulder, *Sam* from the heart to the right leg, *Ham* from the heart to the left leg, *Ksham* from the heart to the moúth.

To us it may seem extraordinary that intelligent persons can give credence to such absurdities, or lend themselves to the practice of superstitions so senseless; but we must bear in mind that with many Hindū thinkers the notion of the eternity of sound—as propounded in Patañjali's Mahābhāshya (I. 1. 1) and in the Pūrva-mīmānsā of Jaimini—is by no means an irrational doctrine. According to the well-known Mīmānsā aphorisma (I.1. 18-23), sound is held to have existed from the beginning. Hence the letters of the alphabet, being the ultimate instruments by which sounds are uttered and thoughts expressed, are considered to possess supernatural qualities and attributes and to contain within themselves an occult magical efficacy.

Let a man only acquaint hemself with the proper pronunciation and application both of the Mantras and of their. Bījas or radical letters, and he may thereby propitiate the Śaktis so as as to acquire through them superhuman power (siddhi)—nay, he becomes, through their aid, competent to accomplish every conceivable object.

At the same time it is to be observed that for any ordinary man to make himself conversant with the Mantras is no easy task; if at least we are to believe a statement in the Tantras that the primary Mantras are seventy millions[18] in number, while the secondary are innumerable.

This, no doubt, is an absurd exaggeration; but it must be borne in mind that only a certain number are regarded as efficacious, and that in the present day there are Brāhmans called Mantra-śāstrīs who make a knowledge of these Mantras their peculiar business, learning them by heart with the sole object of using them as spells and charms. Only a few, however, are believed to have acquired perfect mastery over the most powerful Mantra, which must be pronounced according to certain mystic forms and with absolute accuracy, or their efficacy is destroyed. Indeed, this kind of craft, though supposed to endow the possessor of it with very enviable omnipotence, is not unattended with unpleasant risks and drawbacks; for if in the repetition of a Mantra the slightest mistake is made, either by omission of a syllable or defective pronunciation, the calamity which it was intended to bring down on an enemy will inevitably recoil on the head of the repeater. Then, again, there are various methods of constructing or neutralizing the effect of Mantras used by Mantraśāstrīs for the destruction or humiliation of others. The difficulty, of course, is to find out the exact Mantra which is being employed for one's injury; but, having done so, every such Mantra is rendered powerless by uttering it with one's face bending over a vessel full of milk and then swallowing the milk, or by writing it on the leaf of a banian tree and throwing the leaf into a river [19].

It must be noted, too, that Mantras are not always repeated without a knowledge of their meaning, though the meaning is of little importance compared with the magical force of the letters and sound. Their efficacy also is greatly increased if thev are employed on lucky days or at particular times and seasons. One Tantra teaches that Mantras should be repeated in the month Caitra to give valour; in

Vaiśākha to obtain jewels; in Māgha for intelligence; on Sundays for wealth; on Mondays for tranquillity; on Tusdays for long life, and so on. The intercalary month ought always to be avoided[20]. A few translations of common Mantras[21] are here given:—

'Cause stupefaction (stambhana) of the enemy, paralyze his mouth and tongue; confuse his senses, arrest his speech.'

'Om—reverence to the Lord—svāhā. Let everything be auspicious; let everything opposed to me perish; let everything be favourable.'

'Let Brahmānī, Māheśvarī, Kaumārī, Indrāṇī, Cāmuṇḍā, Vārahī, and Vaishṇavī protect my head, mouth, neck, hands, heart, waist and feet, together with my whole body; protect me, O great goddess, Bhadra-Kālī.' This Mantra is worn as a kavaca or amulet; see p. 204.

'I invoke Bhavānī, accompanied by her husband, attended by her subordinates, by her retinue, by her power (sa-śaktikā), by her vehicle, by her weapons, and by all defensive things.'

'Salutation to the god of love (Kāma-deva) with his five arrows:—the arrow that puts to flight (drāvaṇa-bāṇa); the arrow that enchants (sammohana); the arrow that fascinates (vaśīkaraṇa); the love-kindling arrow (sandīpana); the love-inflaming arrow (santāpana).'

The Gāyatrī or holiest text of the Ṛig-veda is of course the most potent of all Mantras. It is not surprising, therefore, that many Mantras employed by the Śāktas are composed after the model of that text. The following are translations of Gāyatrī Mantras:—

'We meditate on that being who has ashes for weapons; we think of that being who possesses sharp teeth; let our fever (jvara) incite him.' This is called the fever-gāyatrī.

'We meditate on the goddess of nectar; we think of the goddess of love (Kāmeśvarī); let our affection incite him.' This is called the nectar-gāyatrī.

'We meditate on the lord of water (Jaleśvara), we think of the fish-net; let the fish (mīna) incite him.' This is called the fish-gāyatrī.

'We meditate on that being who has a snare for snaring animals; we think of the act of cutting off the victim's head (Śiraś-cheda); let our offering (bali) incite him.' This is called the bali-gāyatrī.

No magician, wizard, sorcerer or witch whose feats are recorded in history, biography, or fable, has ever pretended to be able to accomplish by incantation and enchantment half of what the Mantra-śāstrī claims to have power to effect by help of his Mantras. For example, he can prognosticate futurity, work the most startling prodigies, infuse breath into dead bodies, kill or humiliate enemies, afflict any one anywhere with disease or madness, inspire any one with love, charm weapons and give them unerring efficacy[22], enchant armour and make it impenetrable, turn milk into wine, plants into meat, or invert all such processes at will. He is even superior to the gods, and can make gods, goddesses, imps and demons carry out his most trifling behests. Hence it is not surprising that the following saying is everywhere current in India:—'The whole universe is subject to the gods; the gods are subject to the Mantras; the Mantras to the Brāhmans; therefore the Brāhmans are our gods[23].'

Often these Mantra-śāstrīs are mere professional fortunetellers. I may mention as an illustration that a Śākta Brāhman of this type came to see me one day at Patna. He asked to look at my hand, and, after examining it for a minute, prophesied that my stay in India would be happy and prosperous, except that day fortnight I should meet with a great disappointment. I smiled at the absurdity of his attempting to forecast my future biography, but it is certain that I only met with one unexpected and most mortifying contretemps from the day of my departure from England to the day of my return, and that happened on the very day predicted. It must at least be acknowledged that the coincidence was remarkable.

I may also give an outline of a story told to me by a Marāṭha Pandit, which well illustrates the sort of use these Mantra-śāstrīs are supposed to make of their magical powers. A certain Śākta Brāhman, named Bhāskarācārya, well-versed in the Mantras, expected to be asked to a dinner-party given by a wealthy friend, but received no invitation. This so irritated the Brāhman that he determined to revenge himself on the householder who had ventured so imprudently to slight him. Having waited till the moment when the assembled guests, with appetites stimulated by the fragrance of an array of choice dishes, were about to feast on the delicacies prepared for their consumption, he quietly in his own house selected a paraticular Mantra, and by simply repeating it turned all the viands into foul and fetid excrementitious matter. The story goes on to relate how the householder, suspecting the cause of this disastrous metamorphose, sent a messenger in not haste to implore the immediate presence of the offended Brāhman, who thereupon becoming mollified, obligingly consented to repeat another Mantra which reconverted all the filth into the most delicious ambrosial food.

We now pass on to the Yantras. These are mystical diagrams drawn on metallic tablets, often of copper—generally combinations of the triangular figures like the inverted triangles of the Freemasons—supposed to possess occult powers.

Each of the goddess worshipped by the Śāktas has a

Yantra assigned to her which is sometimes placed in the centre of a lotus-diagram, the Bīja belonging to the goddess being also inscribed a certain number of times on each petal.

The Śrī-Cakra or holy circle is delineated in a diagram of this kind and then worshipped. It is supposed to represent the orb of the earth, nine triangles being drawn within the circle to denote the nine continents. In the centre is the drawing of a mouth, which is believed to typify the female energy (Śakti) presiding over the circle. According to some authorities, even the orthodox Śaṅkarācārya must have been a Śakti worshipper; for he is known to have placed a representation of the Śrī-cakra in each of the four monasteries founded by him.

These Yantras or mystic diagram are thought to be quite as effective in their operation as the Mantras, and of course a combination of the two is held to be absolutely irresistible. An enemy may be killed or removed to some other place, or a whole army destroyed, or salvation and supreme felicity in a future state obtained by drawing a six-sided or eight sided diagram and writing a particular Mantra underneath. If this be done with the blood of an animal[24] killed sacrificially in a place where corpses are burned (Śmaśāna), no power in earth or heaven can resist the terrific potency of the charm. Triangular, pentangular, and nine-triangled Yantras are equally efficacious.

Let us pass to a brief explanation of the Kavacas. I need not tell Sanskṛit scholars that the word kavaca properly means a kind of cuirass, breast-plate, or similar armour worn as a defence in battle. With the Śāktas a kavaca is an amulet or talisman worn as a preservative against evil influences, or to bring about the attainment of some desired object. It may consist of a stone, piece of paper, metal, leaf or other material on which Mantras, Yantras, mystical words and formulæ of various kinds are inscribed. It is then worn on the neck, breast, arms, or loins, especially in times of pestilence and sickness. Women often wear kavacas with the object of propitiating the goddess, and so inducing a condition of body favourable to the producting of male offspring.

The term kavaca is also applied to whole hymns when they are used as charms.

As to the Nyāsas, these consist in mentally assigning various parts of the body to the protection of tutelary presiding deities, with imposition of the hand or fingers, and repetition of texts, mystical words, and syllables.

The Mudrās, on the other hand, are intertwinings of the fingers supposed to possess an occult meaning and to have extraordinary efficacy. Their use as well as that of the Nyāsas will be more fully explained in treating of the morning and evening religious services called Sandhyā.

It may be noted here that four days, or rather nights, are kept as principal festivals by the left-hand worshippers:—namely, (1) the night of the Kṛishṇa-janmāshṭamī (see note 2, p. 113), called the Kāla-rātri; (2) the Moha-rātri or Kālìcaturdaśī, kept on the fourteenth day of the second half of Āśvina; (3) the Śiva-rātri or Mahā-rātri, kept on the fourteenth of the dark half of Māgha; (4) the Dāruṇī Rātriḥ, kept on the day before the Holi festival, which is on the fifteenth day of the first half of Phālguna. But besides these four festivals, nine nights in each of the months Āśvina, Caitra, Pausha, and Āshāḍha are also observed as holy nights. It is declared that ceremonies performed on any of these nights must of necessity confer superhuman power (siddhi).

Before concluding this part of our subject, it may be well to note a few more particulars in regard to the works we have so often quoted as the chief authority for the doctrines and practices of the Śāktas.

The Tantras, I repeat, are the bible of Śāktism. Like the Purāṇas, they are sometimes called a fifth Veda. Very commonly, too, the name Āgama is given to them in contradistinction to Nigama, which is a general name for the Vedas, Dharma-śāstṛas, Purāṇas, and other smṛiti works. Sometimes the authorship of the Tantras is attributed to Dattātreya, who is worshipped as an incarnation of Brahmā, Vishṇu, and Śiva, but the more general opinion is that they were revealed by Śiva alone. None of them have as yet been printed or translated in Europe. They are said to be sixty-four in number, without counting a large collection of works of a Tāntrik character Śākta tendency. As a general rule they are written in the form of a dialogue between the god Śiva and his wife; and every Tantra ought, like a Purāṇa, to treat of five subjects—the creation, the destruction of the world, the worship of the gods, the attainment of superhuman power, and the four modes of union with the Supreme Spirit. In some of the Tantras it is stated that five Āmnāyas or sacred systems of teaching have been handed down from primeval times, one having issued from each of Śiva's five mouths. as a matter of fact very few conform to any systematic arrangement. Those I have examined seem to be mere hand-books for the practices I have attempted to describe, which to Europeans appear so monstrous that the possibility of any persons believing in their efficacy seems in itself almost incredible.

Whole Tantras teach nothing but various methods of making use of spells for acquiring magical power.

Some give collections of charms for making people enamoured, for destroying enemies and rivals, for producing or preventing diseases, for curing blindness, for injuring crops. Others simply describe the most effectual modes of worshipping the Śaktis, Mahā-vidyās, Mātṛis, Yoginīs, Vaṭukas, or by whatever name the innumerable manifestations of Śiva and his wife may be called. Others confine themselves to an explanation of the Yantras, Bījas, and Mudrās (intertwining of the fingers) belonging to each manifestation, the places suited for the worship of each, the names of trees and plants sacred to each, or permeated by each, and the days of the year allotted to each. Some few touch on nearly every conceivable topic of human knowledge, and contain here and there really interesting matter.

Even alchemy comes in for a snare of attention; but the Śākta idea of this pretended science (Rasāyana, Raseśvaravidyā) is that its only use is to enable the devotee to transmute the decaying particles of his body into an incorruptible substance by means of elixirs compunded of mercury and mica, supposed to consist of the essences of Śiva and his wife Gaurī respectively. After long persistence in the practice of swallowing these elixirs the candidate for beatitude becomes immortal, and not merely united with Śiva but identified with him. This kind of transubstantiation is called Jīvanmukti, 'salvation during life[25].'

So little is known about the composition of the Tantras that it is not possible to decide at present as to which are the most ancient, and still less as to the date to be assigned to any of them. They are all said to be founded on the Kaulopanishad. It may, however, be taken for granted that the extant treaties are, like the extant Purāṇas, founded on older works; and if the oldest known Purāṇa is not older than the sixth or seventh century, an earlier date can scarcely be attributed to the oldest known Tantra. Perhaps the Rudrayāmala is one of the most deservedly esteemed and most encyclopedic in its teaching[26]. Others are the Śakti-saṅgama, Viṣva-sāra, Māhā-nirvāṇa, Vīra, Kulārṇava (a text-book of the Kaulas), Śyāmā-rahasya, Śāradā-tilaka, Uḍḍīsa, Kāmākhyā, Vishṇu-yāmala.

Full as the above works are of doubtful symbolism, they are not all necessarily full of impure allusions, though the teaching contained in the best of them unquestionably tends towards licentiousness. When they are better known, their connection with a distorted view of the Sāṅkhya philosophy, and with some of the corrupt forms of Buddhism, will probably be made clearer. Doubtless they have greatly influenced the later Buddhist literature of Nepāl, and would probably throw much light on the magical hymns and spells of the Atharva-veda.

There are also works called Vaishṇava Tantras, such as the Gautamīya and the Sanat-kumāra, but even in these Śiva is the narrator and his wife the supposed listener. Moreover their teaching, which makes Rādhā, the wife of Kṛishṇa, take the place of Durgā as the chief object of adoration, has the same tendency as that of the other Tantras, and equally leads to licentiousness.

Happily the abominations of Śāktism are gradually dying out in British India; and without doubt its true character has long since forced itself on the convictions of the more highly educated Hindūs.

Nor can the power of the Mantra-śāstrīs stand against the moral and intellectual revolution which is slowly but surely upheaving the whole fabric of superstition. That power is already much weakened, and the field for its exercise among a people steeped for centuries in debasing and degarding religious and social ideas is daily becoming narrower. Still in most of the native States, where all the grosser forms of Hindūism are still rampant, the whole system is an firmly established as ever. Even those in high positions, who have no faith in it themselves, find themselves unable to offend the prejudices of their subordinates by venturing to engage in any work or perform the most ordinary act without the sanction of crafty Brāhmans claiming divine authority and professing to work miracles through their knowledge and application of the Mantras.

Well may the enlightened Brāhman so often before quoted give expression to his indignation thus:—

'All sensible people ought to say to the Mantra-śāstrīs, We have suffered much misery through your deceit, we have been taxed very heavily by you, and you have involved us in the results of all your wickedness. It is true your ancestors had some knowledge of different sciences and imparted some of that knowledge to us. In return for these benefits we have fed you and supported you and promoted your interests. When you found your power established over us you abandoned the duty of seeking after knowledge, and worked only mischief. Your teaching is now a mere reflection of your ignorance, wickedness, folly, and hypocrisy. You harass and injure us in a thousand ways. If our knowledge increases, you try to prevent it, thinking that, if inquiry is encouraged, your customers will decrease. We begin to see through your artifices. Begone, every one of you, and don't attempt to deceive us any more.'

Foot Note

1. Sometimes spoken of as plural.
2. Dr. Muir shows this (Sanskṛit Texts, V. 337), and points out that Lakshmī is once used for good-fortune in Ṛig-veda X. 71. 2, and that in Atharva-veda VII. 115. 1 a plurality of Lakshmīs is spoken of. At Madura I noticed carvings of eight different Lakshmīs who preside over different kinds of good-luck. They are often found over the doors of houses.
3. According to Pāṇini II. 2. 34 (Kāśika Vṛitti) the more honourable should stand first in a compound, as in Mātā-pitarau, Śraddhā-medhe, Brāhmaṇa-Kshatriya-Viṭ-Śūdrāḥ.
4. They are more fully describe at the end of this chapter; see p. 205.
5. The wives of all the deities are placed on their left whenever they are represented in juxtaposition. The only exception is in representations of the marriage cremony. On that occasion the bride takes her station on the right of the bridegroom.
6. Some lists give nine Mātrikās (*viz*. 1. Nārashiṇhi , 2. Cāmuṇḍa; 3. Vārahī; 4. Vāruṇī; 5. Lakshmī; 6. Kālī; 7. Kāpālī; 8. Kurukulyā; 9. Indrāṇī), some sixteen, and some fifty-two, among whom are enumerated Nārāyaṇī, Kaumārī, Aparājitā, Durgā, Maheśvarī, etc.
7. All my extracts from the Tantras are taken from the Hon. Rao Bahādur Gopāl Hari Deshmukh's work called Āgama-prakāśa, where the original Sanskṛit of all the passages quoted in this chapter will be found
8. The images of Kālī at Calcutta represent her trampling on her husband. The explanation of this is that she had a contest with Rāvaṇa for ten years, and, having conquered him, became so elated and danced so energetically that Universe would have collapsed under her movements had not Śiva mercifully interposed his body. When the goddess found that she was treading on her husband's sacred person, she suddenly ceased dancing, and, as is not unusual with Hindū women when struck with horror or shame, protruded her red tongue

in a manner not altogether consonant with European ideas of womanly dignity.

9. The Tantras make no secret of the fact that the virile *retas* itself is regarded as the offering most pleasing to the goddess.

10. Another name for an uninitiated person is Kaṇṭaka, 'a thorn.'

11. The verse cited as the authority for the temporary suppression of caste at these meetings is as follows:— Prāpte hi Bhairave cakre sarve varṇā dvijātayaḥ Nivritte Bhairave cakre sarve varṇāḥ pṛithak pṛithak. 'On entering the circle of Bhairava, all castes are on an equality with the best of the twice-born; on leaving it, they are again separated into castes.'

12. The five acts are called the five. Ma-Kāras, because the letter M begins each Sanskṛit word. 'The assemblage of five things beginning with the letter M,' says one of the Tantras, 'satisfies the gods.'

The term Mudrā, which here means fried grain, is also used to denote mystical intertwinings of the fingers.

13. This is well shown by Rājendralāla Mitra in one of his Essays on the Indo-Āryans. The reason given for the cessation of the custom of wine-drinking among the Hindūs is that wine and spirituous liquors were on two particular occasions cursed by the gods Śukra and Kṛishṇa. The cause of Śukra's curse is related in the First Book of the Mahābhārata (ch. 76). It appears that Kaca, son of Vṛihaspati, had become a pupil of Śukra Ācārya with a view to learn from him the charm (mantra) for restoring dead men to life, which none else knew. The Asuras came to know of this, and, dreading lest the pupil should obtain, and afterwards impart, the great secret to the Devas, assassinated him, and mixed his ashes with the wine drunk by his tutor, thus transferring him to the bowels of Śukra Ācārya. It happened, however, that during his pupilage Kaca had won the affection of Devayānī, the youthful and charming daughter of Śukra Ācārya, and that lady insisted upon her father's restoring the youth to her, threatening to commit suicide if the request was not granted. Śukra, unable to deny any favour to his daugher,

repeated the charm, and forthwith, to his surprise, found the youth speaking from his own stomach. The difficulty now was to bring the youth out, for this could not be accomplished without ripping open his tutor's abdomen. Śukra Ācārya thereupon taught the youth the great charm, and then allowed himself to be ripped open, and Kaca, in grateful acknowledgment for his own restoration to life, immediately repeated the Mantra and resuscitated his tutor. But Śukra Ācārya, seeing that it was spirituous liquor which had made him swallow the ashes of his pupil, and that pupil a Brāhman, prohibited for ever afterwards the use of any kind of strong drink by Brāhmans. 'From this day forward,' said he, 'the Brāhman, who, through infatuation, drinks arrack (surā) shall lose all his religious merit. The wretch shall be considered guilty of the sin of killing Brāhmans, and be condemned in this as well as in a future world.'

With regard to the curse pronounced by Kṛishṇa on all spirituous liquor, the reason assigned for it is that his kinsmen the Yādavas had brought great trouble on themselves by their potations.

14. It is said that even in the present day it is not uncommon for the adherents of the Śākta sect to sprinkle spirituous liquor instead of water on the liṅga of Śīva.
15. See Vishṇu-purāṇa.
16. The Taittirīya-brāhmaṇa mentions various ceremonies at which cattle had to be sacrificed. all this is well shown by Dr. Rājendralāla Mitra.
17. The same number is given in the Śaiva-darśana of Mādhava's Sarva-darśana-saṅgraha.
18. Full directions are given in the Tantra-sāra.
19. The Tantra-sāra gives full directions on this subject.
20. The original Sanskṛit text of these, as of all the extracts from the Tantras, will be found in Gopāl Hari Deshmukh's Āgama-prakāṣa.
21. Warlike weapons when thus charmed were supposed to possess supernatural powers and to assume a kind of divine personality like the genii of the Arabian Nights Certain spells had to be learnt for their restraint as well as for their use. When once let loose, he only

who knew the secret Mantra for recalling them could bring them back.

22. The Sanskṛit version of this saying is given incorrectly by Dubois. I have heard it variously rendered. Perhaps the following is the most usual:—Devādhīnaṃ Jagat-sarvam Mantrādhīnāṣ-ca Devatāli Mantrāṣ-ca Brāhmaṇādhīnāḥ Brāhmanā mama Devatāḥ.
23. It may give an idea of the depths of superstition and degradation to which Śāktism can lead if we note here that the retas of either male or female is believed to be still more efficacious.
24. One of the systems described by Mādhava in his Sarva-darśana-saṅgraha is called the Raseśvara-darśana, or the system which teaches the use of mercury or quicksilver as a means of strengthening the body and giving it divine stability capable of resisting death and preventing further transmigration. Mercury is said to be named Pāra-da because it gives *pāra*, or the farther shore of Metempsychosis.
25. It is said to consist of 100,000 verses. a section of it, called Jāti-mālā, treating of caste, has been printed at Calcutta.